A Presence
That Disturbs

A Presence That Disturbs

A Call to Radical Discipleship

ANTHONY J. GITTINS

Liguori/Triumph
LIGUORI, MISSOURI

Imprimi Potest:
Richard Thibodeau, C.Ss.R.
Provincial, Denver Province
The Redemptorists

Published by Liguori/Triumph
An imprint of Liguori Publications
Liguori, Missouri
www.liguori.org
www.catholicbooksonline.com

Copyright 2002 by Anthony J. Gittins, CSSp

ISBN 0-7648-0848-6

Library of Congress Catalog Card Number: 2002101752

Scripture citations are taken from the *New Revised Standard Version of the Bible*, copyright 1989 by the Division of Christian Education of the National Council of the Churches of Christ in the USA. All rights reserved. Used with permission.

Printed in the United States of America
06 05 04 03 02   5 4 3 2

To Anthea, Chris, and Nadir
friends, wayfarers, disciples

Contents

Foreword xi

Introduction xv

CHAPTER ONE
Searching for Meaning,
Renewing Discipleship 1

CHAPTER TWO
The Holy Spirit: Advocate,
Comforter, Life-Giver 23

CHAPTER THREE
Imagination, Encounter, Ministry 43

CHAPTER FOUR
Community, Communitas,
and Downward Mobility 69

CHAPTER FIVE
The Disturbing Ministry of Jesus 91

CHAPTER SIX
Mentors and Midwives,
Images of Discipleship 119

CHAPTER SEVEN
Strangers in the Spirit of Jesus 143

Afterword 163

Notes 165

I have learned
To look on nature, not as in the hour
Of thoughtless youth; but hearing oftentimes
The still, sad music of humanity,
Nor harsh nor grating, though of ample power
To chasten and subdue. And I have felt
A presence that disturbs me with the joy
Of elevated thoughts; a sense sublime
Of something far more deeply interfused,
Whose dwelling is the light of setting suns,
And the round ocean and the living air,
And the blue sky, and in the mind of man:
A motion and a spirit that impels
All thinking things, all objects of all thought,
And rolls through all things.

WILLIAM WORDSWORTH (1770–1850)
"TINTERN ABBEY" [1798]
LINES 88FF

Foreword

Over many years it has become increasingly clear to me that those who wish to move forward as disciples of Jesus must do so by way of community, by way of ecumenism and, above all, by way of the Cross, for a theology of Resurrection is also a *theologia crucis*. We do not follow Jesus in isolation: we are social creatures and pilgrims who need the company of other wayfarers. Particularly significant in the lives of those who try to follow Jesus, therefore, are other disciples. They provide inspiration and encouragement, even if they do not physically accompany us on every step of the journey. But disciples are not only members of our own denomination or confession; they are people from a variety of traditions who share a common baptism.

Every baptized Christian is called to be a member of an ecclesial community, the *koinonia* or community of faith. Indeed, we baptized identify ourselves as members of the community of Christ's body on earth: the Mystical Body. This remains true despite the regrettable—indeed scandalous—divisions within Christianity. My own tradition is Roman Catholic, and I write from that perspective. But, as part of a much broader worldwide community of Christians, I also share a common lineage with people of other traditions within Christianity. Thus, this book is by no means only addressed to Roman Catholics; it is consciously written with all fellow Christians in mind.

"Words crack," said T. S. Eliot. Some words seem inherently strained by the load they are required to bear; words like "Church" or "church," "Christian," and "Christianity," are among them. In these pages I have tried to give them a broad meaning, and to indicate whenever a narrower usage is intended. Consequently, my use of "Church" or "the Church" is inclusive rather than exclusive: it embraces all who share a common baptism. The use of "church" or "churches" is more exclusive, referring to a particular tradition or denomination, or even a particular community or congregation.

"Christendom" in these pages refers to a historical and geographical entity, or to the social construct that conventionally allows us to speak of such an entity. The *World Christian Encyclopedia*[1] glosses "Christendom" as "[t]he traditional portion of the world in which Christianity prevail[ed] or which [was] governed principally under Christian institutions." It refers, essentially, to the Old World as it was known and evangelized in the first millennium. To speak of "Christendom" was to speak of Europe or the Holy Roman Empire, and to indicate that official religion was Christianity. It was also to imply "civilized," or "cultured," rather than barbaric or pagan. But between the eighteenth century Enlightenment and the latter part of the twentieth century, forces of rationalism, secularization, and globalization, as well as religious diversity, increasing freedom of religion, and interreligious tolerance, have made "Christendom" an anachronism. Christopher Dawson was already documenting this historical fact in the 1940s.[2]

In this book, the term "Christendom" characterizes the Christian world between the early fourth century and the mid- or late-twentieth century. In the past half century or so, it is not self-evident that most, or even many, people born and raised within the old confines of Christendom are Christian in any sense of the word. "Christendom" as such, no longer exists: today's Christians live in a world that is largely post-Christian and certainly post-Christendom.

This discussion then brings us to the term "Christian": in this work, "Christian" identifies a person who professes the Christian faith in practical action. By contrast, *nominal* Christians are those who may have been baptized but do not choose to express their faith by public worship or as active members of a faith-community. But I also use "Christian" in its widest, inclusive ecumenical sense (and not as a synonym for Roman Catholic), unless the text indicates otherwise.

The title of this book is taken from a line of William Wordsworth, a favorite poet of my youth, and one who wandered the countryside where I spent my formative years. A recent visit to Tintern Abbey, on the borders between South Wales and England, renewed my interest in the poet and focused my attention on the challenge of radical Christian discipleship.

I am grateful to people who have heard me talk about some of the topics in these pages, and who have encouraged me to develop them further. A version of Chapter Two was presented in a series of lectures celebrating the Year of the Holy Spirit at the University of St. Thomas, Houston, Texas, in 1999. Chapters Three and Six originated as workshops for leaders of Roman Catholic religious orders. A very early form of Chapter Five was presented as the keynote address to the St. Bernard Institute of the University of Rochester, in Albany, New York. Chapter Seven is a topic that has intrigued me for many years and on which I have written elsewhere; but it has not appeared in print in this form.

A number of anonymous reviewers offered helpful suggestions, most of which I have incorporated: I acknowledge my gratitude to them. My editor at Liguori, Judy Bauer, provided many considered and helpful comments; the finished work is consequently more coherent than it otherwise would have been. I am grateful for her insights and suggestions. The inadequacies are my own.

FEAST OF SAINT FRANCIS XAVIER, MISSIONARY
JULY 31, 2001

Introduction
A Presence That Disturbs

During the Nazi persecutions, the strongest resistance by Jews was consistently found to come from those who had neither aging parents nor dependent children; these resisters were only responsible for themselves. But they interpreted that to mean they were *free* to offer the greatest resistance on behalf of the Jewish community as a whole.

Every circumcised child was marked for extermination by the Nazis; a generation of Jewish children, identified by the mark of a religious covenant, was violated and destroyed. All the more curious or impressive, then, was that immediately after World War II Jewish survivors of death camps and ghettos sought one another out, married, had children, *and proceeded to circumcise their sons*. Not only did they continue to believe in a future and in the social institution of marriage, they clung defiantly to tradition and to the public mark of circumcision.

As those children grew up, their parents—who earlier had been willing to speak up and even willing to die—now found themselves afraid or ashamed to share their wartime experiences with their children. But in recent years they have once again begun telling their stories—to their grandchildren. After a generation of silent pain, the story of the Holocaust is being told by those who experienced it. These contemporary heroes are only partly so because of their personal bravery; they are heroes and even more because they themselves are living testimonies to human survival and to the survival of hope itself.[3]

In the estimation of Jewish survivors of the *shoah*, life without a strong Jewish identity would be no better than death. Viktor Frankl was among the survivors, and for three years had been a prisoner of Auschwitz. While still in the death camp he wondered whether he would survive. He concluded that unless he could attribute some meaning to his present predicament and to the appalling suffering of those around him, even if he were to survive his life would be unbearably prolonged and ultimately meaningless. Life without meaning is no life at all. He lived until 1997.

Long before Frankl's time the poet Wordsworth, always searching for personal identity and life's ultimate meaning, wrote the poem familiarly known as "Tintern Abbey." He probably did not believe in God in a conventional Christian way; but for him *nature* was almost synonymous with *divinity*. The ruins of this twelfth-century Cistercian monastery evoked in him the "still, sad music of humanity," and he sensed a presence, a brooding spirit animating the empty choir. He wrote:

> *I have learned*
> *To look on nature, not as in the hour*
> *Of thoughtless youth; but hearing oftentimes*
> *The still, sad music of humanity,*
> *Nor harsh nor grating, though of ample power*
> *To chasten and subdue. And I have felt*
> *A presence that disturbs me with the joy*
> *Of elevated thoughts; a sense sublime,*
> *Of something far more deeply interfused,*
> *Whose dwelling is the light of setting suns,*
> *And the round ocean and the living air,*
> *And the blue sky, and in the mind of man:*
> *A motion and a spirit that impels*
> *All thinking things, all objects of all thought,*
> *And rolls through all things.*[4]

These lines, written in 1798, have power to disturb and challenge even today. Exactly two hundred years later, in 1998, I traveled to the Wye valley, bound for Tintern Abbey. Pillaged for its treasures and its lands in the 1530s by order of King Henry VIII, it now sits silent as a skull with staring, vacant eyes. One wet and misty morning when nothing stirred, I sat within the ruined cloister of this mausoleum and reread Wordsworth's lines. Such was the morning or such the mood, I too felt "a presence that disturbs."

Reflecting on the course of my own life, I was aware that I too had "learned to look on [God], not as in the hour of thoughtless youth." I too had heard, many times "the still sad music of humanity" with its "ample power to chasten and subdue." And that morning, in the still, damp air, I too could sense with the poet, "a motion and a spirit that impels all thinking things." Wordsworth could not have named it, other than as a vague emanation of nature, perhaps a source of meaning; for me it was almost palpably the presence of the Holy Spirit.

Two centuries later, people are still capable of being creatively disturbed by the "still, sad music of humanity." Within living memory, heroism rose from the ashes of the Nazi persecution and expressed itself in the lives of Jews who clung defiantly to their tradition; and two generations after Auschwitz, experience bears out Viktor Frankl's carefully considered prognosis: that if we can discover a meaning amid life's vicissitudes, even a painful existence can be bearable and productive. This is what he spent a lifetime trying to exemplify and to teach. His legacy can be summarized in three neat aphorisms of his own: *to live you must choose; to love you must encounter; to grow you must suffer.*[5] Such is the wisdom of the biblical tradition Christians and Jews are heirs to; such is this legacy that is worth examining again.

To live you must choose. Some people seem to let life happen to them, at best reacting to the daily round rather than taking initiatives. The Jewish-Christian tradition has always set great store by the human capacity for choice: we do not only need to react, we can choose to act, and even choose to accept or reject some of the things that come our way. In the book of the Law, we read of God setting life and prosperity, death and doom, before the people, and urging them to choose wisely: "Choose life so that you and your descendants may live" (Deut 30:19). Despite the cruel suffering of the *shoah*, which included the extermination of members of his own family, Frankl chose to choose life. It is the only way to really live.

To love you must encounter. Some people *know about* many things and many people: they claim to know about the people of Africa or South America, about the poor or about those incarcerated in prison. Such knowledge is legitimate, intellectual knowledge, or what we call general knowledge; but other people actually know people from Africa or South America, actually know poor people or people in prison. This is empirical or experiential knowledge. We cannot truly know, much less love, in the abstract. Frankl identified human encounter as the only authentic way to know and to love. Jesus, of course, exemplified the same idea. The point needs to be repeated for many of us who may be dedicated to people but prevented from real encounters by the structure and shape of our lives. If administration keeps us at arm's length from those whose interests it is intended to serve, then we may need to recall Frankl's simple axiom, and frequently. Encounter is the only way to love.

To grow you must suffer. At first blush this sounds perverse, yet suffering is an essential component of human development. When we encounter suffering that we are unable to remove, we can either turn in upon ourselves and become overwhelmed by it, or we can attempt to turn ourselves and our suffering "inside out." In this way suffering can help us grow. Then it can become redemptive. We may have visited a friend in the terminal stages of illness, only to have come away unexpectedly elevated and encouraged rather than dispirited and discouraged. This type of experience confirms that suffering, nobly borne and not used to evoke sympathy, is one of the strongest faces of the human spirit. Appropriate acceptance of what we cannot change is not only enriching for the sufferer but is a gift of dignity, integrity, and hope to the wider community. Paradoxically, suffering accepted in this way can be life-giving for many.

Two millennia after the Incarnation, the prospect before many people is a little like the view of Tintern Abbey on a misty morning: there is lack of clarity, there is dereliction, there is broken-ness—an alien growth encroaches on sacred precincts. Yet the very ruins hold a memory of what once was; they still have power to evoke "a presence that disturbs." Here perhaps is a metaphor for our lives. It is reiterated in the story of the Holocaust and the Jews who survived. We must discover a reason for living and choose a life worth living to the full. Unless we do, not only are our own lives compromised, we may leave no legacy to those who follow us. Some of us—like the Holocaust survivors who had neither aging parents nor dependent children—may thereby be more free to contribute to the common quest for meaning and purpose. But all of us are challenged, as were the Jewish people, to react to history as it unfolds, to act upon life itself in order to find something meaningful in our human experience, and to forge meaning from the raw material of our lives.

Wordsworths's life was deeply influenced by his encounter with an almost personified Nature and, in turn, he became a lover of nature and a devotee of the quiet life. Every true follower of Jesus is profoundly affected by an encounter with God and, in response, radical Christians become lovers of humanity and rather more socially active than the poet. Therefore, no authentic disciple can be satisfied with a comfortable, private "me-and-Jesus" relationship. And no Christian can attempt to influence others' lives, much less presume to preach to them, unless he or she has first experienced a relationship with the God of Jesus Christ.

Authentic Christianity is marked by a centrifugal force or impulse: it is outreaching and encountering; it communicates and it ministers; it cannot do otherwise. In other words, the test of true discipleship is the experience of something analogous to what Wordsworth felt: *a presence that disturbs.* For disciples, this disturbing presence is the God who both stabilizes and destabilizes, comforts and discomforts. Christianity, like its sibling, Judaism, does not produce complacency, but complicity or participation with others. Therefore we are not permitted to settle for a comfortable symbiosis with nature or even the quiet life. Disciples are challenged to go beyond the experience so tellingly captured by Wordsworth: they must not only have *felt* a presence that disturbs; to be true disciples they must actually *become* a presence that disturbs. This disruption is simply the cost of discipleship. Every disciple is called to practice justice. That call is bound to be disturbing to some people.

Our approach will be to walk in the footsteps of Viktor Frankl (who calls us to choose, to encounter, and to suffer, in order to discover meaning in life) and to remember the lesson of Jewish resistance to the *shoah*. Some of us have become afraid or ashamed to tell our children—biological, adopted, or metaphorical—the story of our lives. Perhaps there is still time for us to recover our nerve, to rediscover our hope, and to find the words to share our faith with our grandchildren.

CHAPTER ONE

Searching for Meaning, Renewing Discipleship

THE SEARCH FOR MEANING

The first televised moment of the third millennium was broadcast from an atoll in the Republic of Kiribati, situated on the equator and snug against the International Date Line. A flaming torch was passed between an older man and a young boy, and carried on the midnight ocean in the safe embrace of a canoe. Few people had even heard of Kiribati, but the commentators quickly learned to pronounce it correctly (keer'-uh-bahs'); and soon the world would have a memory of the night that straddled two millennia.

The opening years of a new century is as good a time as any to evaluate the prospects for contemporary Christianity. Introspective people might look back on other beginnings; optimists might see the blazing promise of a new day, while idealists might sense a splendid opportunity to make a difference. At such a juncture, age-old questions tend to recur: "Who are we?" "Where are we bound?" "What are we doing?" "Why?" Standing on the bridge between two centuries—and, exceptionally, between two millennia—the temptation to look back at the road already traveled, to discern its direction and its contours, is almost irresistible. There seems to be a human compulsion to interpret, to make sense, to discover meaning or to impose it on our unfolding lives and on the events that shape them. Looking back can either degenerate into wistful and wasteful nostalgia or provide important clues about how we came to be where we are. There can be great value in a reflective survey of our lives, one that would help us take the next forward step. Such a survey might disclose for us the hand of Providence that has sustained us in our journeys. We may then be inspired to undertake a course correction for our lives.

Human beings are not generic but specific, particular. Those fortunate enough to have a strong personal identity, individual and social, seem able to diversify, to stretch their cultural wings, and to ride the thermal drafts that carry them to other worlds. Other people seem only to scrape through childhood and adolescence with little or no sense of their own identity or potential. Theirs is a constant struggle to discover meaning and to establish significant relationships.

Christians, of course, are not exempt from this struggle. Many people of faith experience a deep sense of dissatisfaction or *disease* in their lives. Living in the rich countries, enjoying education and employment, taking personal freedom and civic safety for granted, they nevertheless feel something akin to the restlessness Saint Augustine spoke of: there *must* be something more, for indeed "our hearts are restless until they rest in God." Even formal membership in a parish or congregation often fails to satisfy, due to internal bickering or pettiness, or concerns that just seem so *parochial*—so limited to the parish bank balance or to congregational self-interests. Such restlessness is certainly not new, but at this point in history perhaps it can be addressed in a new and life-giving way.

All the mainline Christian denominations are struggling with membership, and most acknowledge that even if they have encouraging numbers of Easter baptisms, they are also losing at least as many active members each year as they acquire. In recent decades, millions of people have ceased to be active worshipers or committed members of a Christian faith community. Some, with grim humor, call themselves "recovering Catholics" or something similar, but many are simply anonymous Christians in a way that Karl Rahner never imagined. Yet there are others (and I am thinking particularly of Roman Catholics here) who want to belong, who want to worship, but who feel battered and betrayed. They experience a highly centralized and authoritarian ecclesiastical institution that does not hesitate to lay down the law, while many of its ministers are being exposed as hypocrites, professionally incompetent, or simply lacking credibility. They feel cheated by a religion with a superabundance of doctrines but a sad lack of compassion. They feel angered by an organization that they fault for having failed to bring hope to millions and having failed to teach love by loving; instead, they charge it with promulgating law and legalism. They feel depleted by the behavior of reactionary authority that constantly adjudicates on liturgical minutiae and private behavior but seems impervious to charges of authoritarianism, high-handedness, and palpable lack of trust. They feel outraged by a system in which sexism, centralization, hierarchy, and exclusion are often more evident than service, dialogue, equality, and inclusion. Sowing formalism, institutional Roman Catholic Christianity is reaping a harvest of resistance and dissent among the faithful. Other denominations are by no means exempt, but currently the Roman Catholic Church is in crisis, and untold numbers of Roman Catholics are deeply disturbed.

The eminent and much-respected British theologian Charles Davis noted that in two generations (between the mid- and late-twentieth century), historical-geographical Christendom collapsed, seemingly healthy Christianity withered on the vine, and the faith and practice of many ordinary people was replaced by a neopagan materialism. This sad experience, shared by myriad contemporaries born and raised as practicing Christians of different denominations in an apparently stable world and church, is not just a personal disaster but has contributed to a cumulative loss of confidence and a deepening sense of disillusion in the wider community.

If institutional Christianity in the broadest sense has failed to deliver on its promises, what alternatives are there? We have seen both a hemorrhage from Christian churches and a yearning (some would say "fad") for "spirituality," as well-intentioned people try their hand at reassembling a fragmented framework of meaning (what sociologists call a "plausibility-structure") for their lives. What hopes are there now for conventional Christianity? What hopes for discipleship that would be more engaged, more radical (*radix, root*), and more life-giving?

In 1910 an international and interdenominational World Missionary Conference took place in Edinburgh, Scotland. By the time it was over it had agreed on a resolution to do everything possible to make the whole world Christian before the year 2000. A century later, that resolution seems as incredible as it was arrogant, as the following five social facts indicate. First, "Christendom" itself (understood in a territorial sense, as the place within which Christianity is the overwhelmingly dominant religion) became increasingly unstable and no longer exists. Second, worship in the traditions of the other world religions is now practiced all over Europe where it used to be banned or hidden. Third, the world religions are as visible as they have ever been. At the same time, though, religionless culture now seems perfectly natural to millions whose parents and grandparents were traditional Christians, whether Roman Catholic, Orthodox, Protestant, or Reformed. Finally, the actual practice of institutional Christianity in all the major denominations is in steep decline. Not only is the contemporary world not Christian, but the Christians of the world are not making the impact that two thousand years of practicing the faith and proclaiming the good news of the gospel had led us to expect. A simple example will illustrate: violation of human rights, civil wars, and structural poverty are an appalling blight on the modern world, yet many (Christian and former Christian) people in the rich nations complain stridently when any increase in foreign aid is mooted. Indeed the question of foreign aid itself is a very sore point; it is widely understood to be optional and a good-will gesture, and few indeed are the nations that consider themselves to have a serious moral responsibility to the people of the poorer countries of the world.

It had been argued, persuasively and well,[6] that as the histori-cally shaped practice of Christianity has gone into steep decline, there has been a parallel trend. The number of people—many of whom are former practicing Christians—voluntarily working for the hospice movement or soup kitchens, charitable organizations or overseas aid agencies, or simply undertaking voluntary work among poor and homeless people, appears to have risen signifi-cantly. It is not always easy to interpret this trend. However, people in the richer nations have a much longer life expectancy than they did a century ago.[7] This demographic change could mean that though the gross number of volunteer hours has increased, the life of the average individual today is actually less marked by voluntary commitment of time and service than in a previous age. What is certain, though, is that compared with half a century ago, far fewer volunteers today offer their services to or through the Christian churches.

Such are some contemporary trends. What hope is there for Christianity, whether ecumenical or denominational, in the post-modern world? What prospects for believing Christians when conventional religion is so compromised? What encouragement for people who endorse many so-called Christian values but find Christianity itself to be a scandal or irrelevance? Perhaps a survey of some current images of God will enable us to identify both stumbling blocks and possible ways forward for contemporary men and women seeking meaning and looking for a star.

GOD AS SUGAR-DADDY

A *sugar daddy* is a rich, older, male figure who overindulges a protégé in return for rather sycophantic service, or worse. There is a hydra-headed and pernicious form of religion with roots in pre-Christian times and branches even in our own: Gnosticism. In its current form, it amounts to a belief that religion is a private affair between individual and God; that each person has all the knowledge (*gnosis*, hence *gnosticism*) needed; and that no one has any business interfering with the way an individual chooses to live. This Gnosticism exhibits certain features of *sugar-*

daddyism, claiming a special arrangement between an individual and God, and even imagining that God can be manipulated.

Though very clearly antithetical to the religion Jesus preached (which was about relationships, social and public responsibility, love, forgiveness, and reconciliation), forms of Gnosticism have survived for more than two thousand years. They may be found today rather comfortably ensconced in the lives of many who call themselves Christians, appearing as a kind of civil religion, the philosophy that endorses the primacy of an individual's entitlements or privileges. Such contemporary Gnosticism assumes that God underwrites whatever seems good to a private individual. It allows people go through life both contented and justified, as long as they do not harm or interfere with anyone else—according, of course, to their own judgment.

This attitude is infectious, and its attendant problems are myriad. It would allow us to reduce God to a caricature, or create God in our own image. Then God can be manipulated and we can continue to feel comfortable. Above all, this God does *not* disturb us. We become the judge in our own case. We become closed to the possibility of being shaken up, challenged, and commissioned by God. We have little or no social conscience; and quite soon we place ourselves beyond the criticism of others and particularly out of earshot of the cries of the poor.

GOD AS RELENTLESS PURSUER

The English poet Francis Thompson (1859–1907) was no stranger to restlessness, and he spoke dramatically about being pursued by God in the guise of *The Hound of Heaven.* His only instinct, he says, was to try to escape:

> *I fled Him, down the nights and down the days;*
> *I fled Him, down the arches of the years;*
> *I fled Him, down the labyrinthine ways*
> *Of my own mind; and in the midst of tears*
> *I hid from him, and under running laughter.*

Increasingly breathless, the poet recounts the futile attempt to hide, the relentless pursuit by God, and his own terror of divine judgment. Thompson, a devoutly religious man and former Roman Catholic seminarian, was at the time of writing addicted to smoking more than three pounds of opium a day. He was sick and suicidal, lamenting the futility of his life and his dashed hopes, yet gifted with that fierce intensity and devastating insight that sometimes marks those judged to be insane. As he senses that the end of the chase is very close, the poet cries out with a sense of terrible sadness at the pathetic mess his life has become—yet with conscious irony:

My days have cracked, and gone up in smoke.

Finally he is caught, but not by the rabid and fearsome hound he feared. It is a gentle, loving father who gathers up this panic-stricken adult-child. And he hears, not words of reproof but words of encouragement as his (Heavenly) father says:

All which I took from thee I did but take
Not for thy harms,
But just that thou might'st seek it in my arms.

By his own judgment, Thompson was a spoiled seminarian and failed physician. He was also mentally ill and a homeless vagrant, a drug addict and a mystic, and shortly before his premature death he discovered the peace and commitment which he had never stopped seeking. His restless heart rested at last in God, the one he famously calls "this Tremendous Lover."

There is something quite compelling in the drama of this poem. Countless people have found inspiration in the poet's odyssey. Yet there is a danger of our romanticizing or sentimentalizing the experience, or of seeing this simply as a "happy ever after" story and of leaving it there. Thompson himself was far from naive, and terribly aware of how the Christ he knew did not only comfort and heal but also challenged and commissioned. At one point in the poem he cries out to God: "Ah! must Thou char the wood ere Thou canst limn with it?" Yet he already knows the answer: the artist cannot create a charcoal sketch unless the green wood has first been burnt,[8] and God cannot fashion true disciples unless there is some discipline in their lives. But the poet knows that Jesus did not merely gather up his loved ones in a warm embrace but sent them forth into a sometimes hostile world as lovers and witnesses: and this is what both makes him so afraid and yet restores his sense of self-worth. The moment of his greatest fear and doubt is also the moment immediately prior to his restoration. Here is the fear:

> *And now my heart is as a broken fount,*
> *Wherein tear-drippings stagnate, spilt down ever*
> *From the dank thoughts that shiver*
> *Upon the sighful branches of my mind.*
> *Such is; what is to be?*
> *The pulp so bitter, how shall taste the rind?*

"The pulp so bitter, how shall taste the rind?" For so many people today, this question is their own: if the privileged life we experience is yet so meaningless, how will we cope when hardship, sickness, and death approach? And here, for Thompson, is restoration. God is speaking:

> *All which I took from thee I did but take,*
> *Not for thy harms,*
> *But just that thou might'st seek it in My arms.*
> *All which thy child's mistake*
> *Fancies as lost, I have stored up for thee at home:*
> *Rise, clasp My hand, and come!*

The gathering-and-accepting-and-restoring movement depicted by the God of *The Hound of Heaven* concludes with the very word of invitation that Jesus extends: "Come!" The challenging-and-empowering-and-commissioning movement of the Jesus of the Gospels is thus the supplement or complement to the poem. It is also what made the poet afraid, because it required a radical response. The Jesus movement is such that those who are called are also sent; those who are loved and forgiven are also inspired to love and to forgive; those who are healed are also dispatched as healers; and those who are disturbed by God's encouraging and enabling presence are also commissioned to be a presence that disturbs. It is a heady, and a heavy, responsibility. Thompson's poem might become the initial part of a reflection on the Christian vocation. We are called to love our neighbor as ourselves; but unless we first love ourselves we are incapable of loving our neighbor. Those who have not experienced love find it impossible to love themselves with any consistency: nor can they love others. Thompson's early life seems not to have been marked by the experience of love or the conviction that he was loved. Only when he had dropped out of medical school and been homeless for several years was he taken in by the poets Wilfrid and Alice Meynell. It was their unconditional love and hospitality that made his rehabilitation possible.

Sometimes Christians act like the stereotypical Pharisees who imposed on others backbreaking burdens that they would not carry and could never have carried themselves. To make impossible demands on others is an act of injustice. Yet some Christians are only too quick to brand certain categories of people as sinners. Genesis House in Chicago[9] is a place of welcome and support for women trying to escape from prostitution. It is a place where many volunteers and employees first began to understand how unjust and unforgiving some Christians and a certain type of Christianity can be. If human beings do not experience love and thus are not yet able to love others, then to judge them guilty of sin is to be guilty of sinful judgments oneself. In fact, if due to abuse or abandonment a person has not experienced love, such a person cannot be morally guilty of failing to love others. The axiom *nemo dat quod non habet* ("one cannot give what one has not first received or possessed") applies as much to love as it does to anything else. To condemn victimized and unloved persons because they do not meet public standards of behavior is to add insult to injury.

Only when Francis Thompson experienced the love of others

was he enabled to love himself. Only then could his self-respect begin to blossom, slowly, painfully, and almost too late. His premature death cut short his spiritual rehabilitation and his growing response to God's enabling grace. Likewise, only when one of the women of Genesis House, "Teddy Bear" by name, broken by abuse, drugs, and prostitution, discovered that she had found a sanctuary where she was accepted unconditionally could she begin to find the peace and healing she craved. But in her case the ravages were too deep, and her broken body could not live with her rekindled spirit. Yet when she died at thirty-one, she did know what it was to love her neighbor because she had at last begun to love herself. She discovered what the poet discovered and what many of us also discover—that we are sometimes our own worst enemies and that we are only too capable of building walls that separate us from the one we most keenly need.

The *Hound of Heaven* concludes with God's tender words:

> *Ah, fondest, blindest, weakest,*
> *I am He Whom thou seekest!*
> *Thou dravest love from thee, who dravest me.*[10]

GOD AS DISTURBING PRESENCE

The image of God as *Hound of Heaven* (pursuing us relentlessly but only to hold us safe in a warm embrace) is ultimately inadequate; people may surrender to God in some sense, without becoming identifiable as fully committed disciples. Even more obviously, the sugar-daddy image of God (benign, uncritical and indulgent supporter of my law-abiding life) is not truly Christian. Our Christian tradition would indeed endorse the image of God as "this Tremendous Lover" who would no more abandon us than a mother would abandon a child; and indeed there is an element of the *Abba* or *daddy* that is quite consistent with our imagining of God. But full-blooded Christianity is not only comforting but very demanding. Just as the God of the *Hound of Heaven* leads us and invites us home—"arise, clasp my hand, and come!"—so our *Abba* not only calls us but sends us as well, as

Jesus himself was called and sent. So we must add to our images of God and acknowledge that God calls in order to send, and heals and restores in order to increase the number of those who will in turn reach out to their brothers and sisters with healing and restoration.

Where might we look for a more helpful and integrated image of God? The idea of God is itself quite dangerous: images of deities (and of Yahweh) were forbidden by the Torah and have been proscribed by iconoclasts ever since, and for good reason. No image can really do justice to Divinity; and any image taken too seriously becomes an idol. Idolatry is mistaking an image of God for the reality it represents. Image-making tends to reduce God to manageable proportions, attempting to "domesticate" God or to subvert God's command. As such, image-making can be naive, pretentious, and deadly.

Yet there is an *aspect* of God, if not exactly an *image*, which has been increasingly emphasized in recent theological writing. It may derive from the profound notion of Emmanuel: God with us. It is God-in-relationship. God-involved with creation, God-of-Covenant, God-of-all-people, God-of-the-poor. A significant development in contemporary theological thinking presents a direct challenge to any naive "me-and-God" piety or privatized faith. As we take the first steps toward a renewed definition of discipleship, increasingly aware of the unfulfilled promise of Christianity (the "not yet" part of the realm of God) and the unfinished agenda confronting any thinking person, our complacency cannot but be shaken and our conscience must be stirred. Given the obscene inequities and the palpable injustice that affects the lives of millions of human beings, we must not allow ourselves to be seduced by the "I'm-all-right-so-long-as-I'm-not-harming-anyone" philosophy. Unless we are actually helping someone we are contributing to injustice by omission and delict. Given the daily impact of forces of globalization on our lives, we simply cannot plead ignorance or continue to be impervious to the cries of the poor. Nor can we limit our own religious journeys to any kind of self-focused spirituality or liken them to a pleasant and leisurely stroll in the woods.

The Second Vatican Council (1962–1965) offered helpful

correctives to a comfortable Roman Catholic Christianity, including the variety that fashioned for itself an image of God as an indulgent father who, having tracked down errant souls, leaves them self-satisfied or indolent. But Vatican II speaks to Christians of all stripes: we *are* the Church; we *are* the body of Christ; we *are* our brothers' and sisters' keepers. And because of our common baptism we simply cannot leave evangelization and justice to others: they are our responsibility too. And they need to be taken rather seriously.

Theologian Johannes Metz has spoken of the legacy of Jesus as a *dangerous memory.* Jesus calls and commissions, but also promises a sword of division (Mt 10:34–36) that will come between people, and a life "not without persecutions" (Mk 10:30). But he also promises that those who persevere to the end will be saved. Jesus certainly disturbs us. Wordsworth's poetic image of "a presence that disturbs" may be better suited to the times in which we live than either Francis Thompson's image of a hound, however heavenly, or the image of a sugar-daddy, however benign.

A TRUE EXPERIENCE OF GOD

Every authentic religious epiphany or encounter, every true experience of God in whatever form, makes a person less insular, less complacent, and less isolated—and more restless, more inspired and more engaged with the world and humanity. Wordsworth captures very well the effect of what Rudolf Otto spoke of as the tremendous and fascinating mystery of the Holy: its awesome power is indeed disturbing, yet it is much more. There seems to be a twofold dynamic at work when one encounters the Transcendent, the Absolute, the Holy, *Nature,* or God. The first movement is perhaps that one is disturbed by the encounter; the second is that one actually becomes an agent of disturbance; that is to say, the encounter is neither a purely private affair (me-and-God, me-and-the-Other) nor are its effects confined within the personal sphere (my-business-and-no-one-else's): the disturbing presence has as one of its effects the power to cause people to become disturbers of the *status quo*. For those who believe in the Spirit of God, the Paraclete—also known as Comforter, Advocate, Defender, or Intercessor—this might be a way of assessing how and where that same Holy Spirit is at work in our day.

Even so, many people seem to pass through life without having encountered God in any meaningful way. Of these, some indeed have an admirably high moral code, both personal and social, and consequently they take pains to rock the boat, upset the applecart, or otherwise create well-intentioned disturbances among their social circles. But others simply pursue their own agendas with little or no awareness of the needs of others or of their own social responsibilities.

Every baptized Christian is, or should be, someone with an actual (disturbing) experience, certainly a close encounter, with God; someone who, as a result, becomes a disturbing presence to others. Is not the Christian someone who, as Dorothy Day is reported to have said, comforts the afflicted and afflicts the comforted under the inspiration of the God of faith? Is not the Christian someone whose heart is restless as long as injustice exists, someone touched or inspired by Divine restlessness, someone who does *not* believe that Christianity is altogether compatible with the quiet life? So how do we identify our social and religious responsibility?

If we think within an ecclesiocentric framework we may assert that Christianity and its multiple churches have a mission. If we think within a narrow egocentric framework we may claim that Christians (individually and collectively) have a mission. But if we expand our framework, both those statements seem wrongheaded, even a little arrogant. If our thinking has God the Creator or Jesus the Savior at its center, then everything looks different. In a theocentric cosmos the mission belongs to God: God *is* mission; just as in a Christocentric world the mission belongs to Christ.

The foundation and origin of mission is God. Jesus is God literally brought down to earth to continue God's mission. As Jesus identifies himself and his work with his *abba* and his *abba's* work, so those who aspire to follow Jesus try to acknowledge that the initiative, the call, and the commission, reside in him. It would be more correct, therefore, to say that God being God and

Jesus being Savior, *the mission has a Church*. In other words, the Church of Jesus Christ (and every constituent Christian church) is an instrument by means of which God's mission is carried out. The Church itself does not have a mission as such; the Church— universal, local, and denominational—*is in the service of God's mission*. By extension, we ourselves, individually and collectively, do not have a mission: the mission has us (congregations, communities, and individual followers of Jesus).

Mission is not a program or a series of rational tasks, however noble these programs or tasks are. It is the extension of God's loving, saving, and redeeming activity and encounter throughout the world by whatever means and in whatever circumstances. Jesus said that his business was to proclaim and bring about the realm or kingdom of God. That concept is so open-ended as to be messy, and therefore is quite frustrating to the tidy-minded. When Jesus announces in the synagogue that "today this scripture has been fulfilled in your hearing" (Lk 4:22), he has just read from the prophecy of Isaiah. The passage describes one of the least programmatic missionary undertakings we could imagine. Rather than a systematic program ("go, teach, baptize") as in Matthew 28:16, there is a general injunction to "bring good news to the poor, to proclaim liberty to captives, [to give] the blind new sight, to set the downtrodden free, and to proclaim the Lord's year of favor." In other words, as followers of Jesus and commissioned by him, we must go *wherever there is need*, encounter *whoever is in need*, and do *whatever it takes* to bring the good news of redemption and liberation.

The spirit identified by Isaiah and claimed by Jesus as underwriting his ministry has become identified by the church with the third Person of the Trinity: the Holy Spirit. This identification allows Vatican II to assert that baptism incorporates every Christian into a missionary community because the same Holy Spirit that inspired Jesus is also given to the baptized. Jesus declared that he was sent to the poor and needy in general, though of course he had to deliberately seek out, encounter, and be encountered by actual people in specific circumstance. In like manner, the mission of Jesus was not restricted[11] except by the limits of his own public life. So we—disciples, missionary Christians—cannot limit our own call and commissioning.

Mission *ad gentes*—to the ends of the earth and to people who have not yet heard the message of Christ—remains an imperative; but mission cannot be focused only on the farthest reaches of the earth since all baptized Christians are to be involved and most cannot possibly engage in mission *ad gentes*. Everyone is called to proclaim—by word or witness, by liberation or through relationships[12]—from the housetops or the streets, from the office or the schoolroom, from the home or the parish: from wherever they happen to be. So mission is not delimited by geography or restricted to certain persons; but it does require flexibility, energy, perseverance, and commitment from all who take their baptism seriously. Mission requires that the disciples be like the master: a disturbing presence; but Christians have not always been faithful—to Christ or to the mission.

A CHANGING UNDERSTANDING OF MISSION

Certain phrases gained wide currency, particularly among Roman Catholics, with Vatican II. Two of the most familiar expression are surely these: "The Church is missionary by its very nature" and "everyone is a missionary by virtue of baptism." However, what may have sounded stunningly innovative in the 1960s has become bland or meaningless for many people at this point in time. If everyone is a missionary, it is sometimes said, then nobody is a missionary; and if everything is mission, then nothing is mission. It may be time to revisit these phrases and their underlying theology.

To assert that the Church is missionary by its very nature is to say something like "all men are born equal" or "human life is sacred": it may be perfectly true in principle without being palpably true at all. The Church universal and the various Christian churches have not always lived up to their own call and commission, any more than human beings have always treated one another with dignity or respect. Similarly, to claim that all Christians are missionary by baptism is certainly not to describe a reality. All

Christians are *called to be, empowered as, commissioned to be* missionaries by baptism; but not all baptized Christians actually do respond, activate that potential, or carry out the commission. Among several possible reasons for this circumstance may be that many who would call themselves Christians have a very strong antipathy toward the very word "missionary," with its connotations (for them) of intensity and even force, joylessness, and a certain grim determination.

From the day of Pentecost (Acts 2) and the beginning of Christianity, followers of Christ understood their responsibility both toward other Christians and fellow Jews, and to Greeks and other pagans. The believers—first called "Christians" in Antioch (Acts 11:26)—were convinced of the Resurrection of Jesus and of his imminent return. They felt impelled to broadcast this Good News, both to a world awaiting the Messiah and to a world beyond where people simply had no idea of a Messiah at all. The impulse was from within (good news cannot contain itself) and from without (Paul's "woe to me if I do not preach the Gospel"). In the early centuries, to be a Christian was both demanding and "cost-effective": very expensive and yet highly desirable.[13] Christians did not have an easy life. Professing the faith was a high-risk occupation. Yet the Christian community grew exponentially during the first three centuries when to be a believer included a missionary attitude and dynamic: Christianity was an evangelizing religion—of proclamation, witness, dialogue and liberation—and Christians took their responsibilities seriously.

By the time Europe had been evangelized—mostly by monks, and largely between the sixth and the tenth centuries—Christianity was the established, mainstream religion. All traditional, local religions—generically referred to as *pagan*—ceased to exist legally. Christianity was the only official religion of Europe; and since Europe and Christianity were now deemed to be coextensive, Europe could now be called *Christendom*. No longer a minority religion, Christianity had less need to assert its identity against competitors. To be a Christian became considerably less demanding and increasingly less cost-effective than it had previously been. But now that it cost less to be a Christian, Christianity also lost some of its countercultural allure and heroic dimensions. No longer was it illegal or risky to be a Christian. In fact, a slow and subtle change had overtaken the steps leading to membership in the Christian community and the nature of Christian practice.[14]

The first generation of disciples actually *knew Jesus*. After the Resurrection and Ascension, new disciples came to *know about Jesus* from those who had known him personally. Gradually, however, membership in the Church became dependent, not on having known Jesus himself, but on *believing in the Creed*. For many centuries now, people have become members of the Christian family through infant baptism and implicit belief in *what the church believes*, even though they may not be very clear about what that actually means. The four stages[15] represent significant shifts. And since *belief* can have as its object a set of propositions, whereas the proper object of faith (actually, its subject) is a relationship (actually, a person), it is now possible to claim to be a Christian (believer) without being a person of faith, something that would have been inconceivable to Saint Paul. Indeed it is arguable that many more people claim to believe in God than to know God experientially—or even to realize that such a possibility exists. Furthermore, the nature of membership of the body of Christ, and thus of involvement and responsibility, had evolved considerably. By the Middle Ages the two estates—clergy and laity—had become increasingly separated and polarized: what God had joined together, humanity was increasingly separating, by gender, hierarchy, social class and religion; and, as this social change continued, religious formalism and the polarization of clergy and laity succeeded in eroding the missionary dimension that had been essential to the self-understanding of generations of Christians.

A CHANGING UNDERSTANDING OF MISSIONARY

The sixteenth century saw both the revisioning of the known world and a wave of protest against the church of Rome. The radical revisioning both generated and followed half a century of voyages of discovery, while the tidal wave of protest produced, in the

Reformation and its aftershocks, the cataclysmic fracture of Christendom. In the fifty years that straddled the year 1500, followers of Henry the Navigator had sailed south from Portugal and had rounded the tip of Africa, while Columbus and those who sailed west "discovered" a New World. As geography was being redefined, so indeed was religion: between 1517 and 1560 Christian Europe—long since scarred by schism and heresy—was now deeply polarized by Lutheran, Presbyterian, and Anglican (Episcopalian) protests against Rome. One consequence was the formation of national Reformed churches in Germany and France, Scandinavia, and the Netherlands, England and Scotland.

This maelstron, however, also produced unexpected benefits. As new lands and their inhabitants were colonized and as ecclesiastical authority was challenged by political power, the rights of indigenous inhabitants and foreign potentates had to be defined. What did it mean to be human; and did the definition include the heretofore unimagined populations? The spiritual and indeed physical fate of millions hung in the balance. It was not until 1537 that a Papal Decree[16] defined the newly encountered populations to be human. This declaration meant, in principle, that these people had rights (though this was still a Hobbesian world where life was often "nasty, brutish, and short" and notions of a social contract as guarantor of human rights were still a century in the future). The decree also, and perhaps even more ominously, meant that the native people could—and must—be baptized.

The borders of Europe had largely been secured for Christianity by the end of the first millennium. If Christianity was to continue to expand, it would now need to move beyond Europe, or Christendom. The "one, true faith" had been opposed by the encroachments of Islam and the resilience of the Jewish faith, and threatened by schism and heresy from within, but it appeared to have survived and indeed to have prospered in Europe. Suddenly at this point—around the year 1500 and on the verge of the Reformation that would result in compound fractures to the body of Christ—there was a New World to be won for Christ. Untold hordes of people were judged to be in danger of damnation and ripe for conversion. In practice, however, the Cross marched with the sword and the flag, oftentimes in step, though sometimes not. The story of the Christianization of the expanded world of the sixteenth century is bittersweet. Heroic and humane undertakings coexisted with exploitation and extermination on a truly unprecedented scale; European civilization (the mission of *civilizing*) became confused with Christian conversion (the mission of *converting*); and rampant ecclesiastical imperialism was often indistinguishable from the worst excesses of political colonialism.

Among the many casualties in this period of dramatic and traumatic change were the missionary movement itself and the missionary dimension of the lives of rank-and-file Christians. It was during the internecine "religious" wars of the sixteenth and early seventeenth century that the implicit unity of Christians was first exposed in all its poverty and then rent apart. For their survival, the various factions of Christianity turned in upon themselves and all but abandoned the centrifugal momentum that had sustained the faith for more than a millennium. The Council of Trent (1545–1563) saw no other option but to issue a clarion call to the Roman Catholic church—"universal" perhaps, but certainly broken—to live up to its missionary responsibilities.

The foundation of the Society of Jesus (1540) represented a new model of Christian commitment to an expanded world. Indeed, with the Jesuits the word "missionary" is actually created. Now there is an elite corps, explicitly dedicated to formal evangelization and the conversion of the newly encountered populations and clearly distinguished from *patronato réal*, the political power exercised by kings as extenders of the boundaries of Christianity. But now, too, a wedge has been driven (in Roman Catholic circles) between "missionaries" and the rest of Roman Catholic Christians. Soon the distinction will be quite strongly emphasized, not simply by virtue of the apostolic lifestyle of the former (a "religious life" of poverty, chastity, obedience within a community), but by their being sent ("co-missioned") beyond the confines of Christendom to the geographical "ends of the earth." Before long, rank-and-file Christians will have forgotten (if indeed any of them even realized) how intrinsic an aspect of Christianity mission had always been. Now some people are called missionaries by virtue of their far-flung ministry and conventual apostolic lifestyle. Such men now regarded themselves as the only true missionaries, and indeed were regarded as such by the rest of the baptized.

A CHANGING UNDERSTANDING OF CHURCH

By 1800, but very gradually, an operative Roman Catholic theology had developed with the following characteristics: the rank-and-file (laity) stay at home and support the missionaries (celibate clergy and male religious) by prayer and almsgiving; and the laity accept this as divinely ordained. The missionary component that was originally an organic part of Christian life thus came to be seen as optional and was allowed to atrophy. In the meantime, "missionaries"—very much in the minority—claimed to be, and were perceived to be, a more perfect and heroic model of the Christian life. The Body of Christ, already fragmented by the Reformation, was becoming even more divided, this time by a horizontal division. Hierarchy rather than equality marks this body, and the Spirit seems to be given disproportionately to the clergy. There appears to be a radical reinterpretation of Saint Paul, who had written: "All the members of the body, though many, are one body....Now *you together* [italics added] are Christ's body; but each of you is a different part of it" (1 Cor 12:12, 27) [second half of quote is from the Jerusalem Bible].

Roman Catholics never completely forgot the missionary dimension of Christianity, though they made it a narrow specialization within the Church. But the churches of the Reformation were no better: it took a considerable time for them to acknowledge the missionary outreach as an essential component of Christianity. With the exception of the pioneer Bartholomäus Ziegenbalg (1682–1719),[17] who went as the first Protestant (Lutheran Pietist) missionary to Asia, who arrived in India in 1706, the earliest missionary enterprise in these churches dates only from the final years of the eighteenth century or the beginning of the nineteenth.

The eighteenth century also represents the low point of Roman Catholic missionary outreach. The missionary flame flickered and almost died. The Jesuits had been suppressed (1767) and the Enlightenment was capturing the European imagination and turning it away from Christian faith and practice. By the time of the Roman Catholic missionary initiative of the nineteenth century, many Reformed churches had established their own missionary societies. In consequence, though that century saw unprecedented missionary initiatives from virtually all of the Christian churches, those initiatives were partly driven by a scandalous spirit of competition and by mutual anathematizing. Members of different Christian denominations rebaptized each other's church members, and the unity for which Christ prayed was even further compromised. The "scramble for Africa"—and the concomitant scramble for Asia and the Pacific—brought out some of the least attractive characteristics of Christian self-righteousness and judgmentalism.

Such is the shifting ground upon which the present age has built. Yet although unsavory behavior is not entirely a thing of the past, within the Christian denominations today there is an admirable ecumenical spirit. But for many people it is too late: the damage has been done.

A mustard seed that grew into a huge tree, Christianity appears to have gone into steep decline since the Enlightenment of the eighteenth century. At the beginning of a new century, there is less enthusiasm for Christian missions among more people in what used to be called Christendom than for most of the previous two thousand years. As the twenty-first century gathers momentum, the credibility and influence of Christianity slows to near inertia. This inactivity is not the first time missionary enthusiasm has waned, but it offers reflective people an opportunity to take stock, to consider the principles on which their lives stand, and to determine whether and how they will respond to a world in dire need.

SUMMARY

The temptation to look back in a search for patterns as pointers for the future is almost irresistible. In this chapter, we have identified the human need for meaning and the crisis of meaning identified by Viktor Frankl and experienced so widely today. We have considered a couple of ways people imagine God (as one who indulges our whims or pursues us until we can no longer resist). We have suggested that however inadequate these may be, meaning can indeed be found, and it comes from our own experience of God. God neither indulges nor hounds us, but God does disturb us, animate us with a sense of mission, and call us to disturb a complacent or confused world.

We have also considered the relative disarray in which the Christian churches find themselves today. And we have noted that the history of Christianity itself contains many seeds that produced tares rather than wheat. We have noted that there are various countercurrents to Christianity and some alternative carriers of meaning. We mentioned the Enlightenment, and noted too that today the spirit of postmodernity declares bleakly that there is no "meta-narrative," no single key to unlock life's meaning, indeed no overall deep meaning to be found anywhere.

Yet all this is not to say that because Christianity has not yet or has not always succeeded it cannot succeed again. It has been said that Christianity remains as a great idea that has never really been tried. But as the modern and postmodern world has failed to deliver the promised Utopias, human beings still continue to look for meaning, still believe in meaning, or still hope for meaning. Some still look to Christianity. For those who do, the following pages may bring some encouragement. These pages will look again for the meaning in the message of Jesus. But first we turn in the direction of the Spirit, whom Jesus promised to be our Advocate, Comforter, and Life-Giver after the Ascension. If our discipleship is to be renewed we must first be Spirit-led. The Spirit of God will help us to discover life's ultimate meaning.

CHAPTER TWO

The Holy Spirit: Advocate, Comforter, Life-Giver

INTRODUCTION

Susan Classen is a Mennonite missionary and a gardener. Lessons she learns from gardening seem to apply directly to her mission. She makes splendid hanging flower baskets, things of beauty. When she first started, she would carefully cut and pare, water and feed, her plants. But after a while they began to wither. She continued to water them but many of her plants died. However, discarded cuttings had fallen to the ground and been fed by the overflow from the daily waterings. As some of the plants in the baskets above were dying, some cuttings in the earth beneath were striking root and flourishing. There *was* life, and gardening skill *was* important. But the life was not where the gardener expected it. And for all her care and commitment, she certainly did not create it.

The lesson is easy to apply. First, our passionate commitment is urgently necessary, but it is God who gives the increase and we must not be tempted to control the Spirit of God who renews the face of the earth. But, second, we need to reflect on the way we

live: on our own expectations and on our own responses to results; on our ability to take initiatives; on our willingness to wait
on God; on our faith and faithfulness.

Every disciple of Jesus is first called to an encounter with
God, and then sent by the Spirit to bring hope and to restore
meaning to other people's lives. But even the suggestion of an
encounter with God comes as a surprise to many of our contemporaries: they seem to have forgotten, or never to have known,
that we are people of the Covenant: people in a historic and con-
tinuing relationship with God. Perhaps they have also forgotten
those ringing words, "Follow me, and I will make you fish for
people" (Mt 4:19), words that apply in principle to all who respond to their baptismal call. The Holy Spirit is Jesus' promised
legacy to the Church, and Christians who recite the Creed claim
to believe that God's Spirit is active in the world. This chapter
goes in search of the Holy Spirit: the *Paraclete* or advocate of
victims; the Comforter; the Elusive One; the One who is able to
disturb us, to galvanize us, and to refocus our lives. But this is a
delicate undertaking, for God's Spirit is invisible to all but the
eyes of faith, silent to all but those who listen attentively, and
overlooked by all but those who live by hope.

Institutional Christianity, at least in the mainline churches,
appears to be slipping away, in T. S. Eliot's words, "not with a
bang but with a whimper." Fifteen or sixteen centuries of bad
habits and irresponsible living have taken their toll: Christendom
(the once-vibrant, energetic body of Christ as it existed throughout the Old World) has aged, become sclerotic and hard of hearing, and is losing its sight. Where is the hope of a *New Pentecost?*
Who are the bearers of *new life?* How healthy is the Body of
Christ today?

It has been suggested that the history of Christianity can largely
be read as the tale of the *defeats* of the Holy Spirit: triumphalism,
imperialism, the use of force, fear, and anathema, are *not* what
God's Spirit had in mind. Among Roman Catholics, as parts of
the institutional church struggle to change appropriately,
"restorationists" redouble their efforts to turn back the clock in
hopes of recovering a mythical Golden Age. But social institu-

tions are not immortal; they must change or die. This may be unthinkable for some people, but the institutional church (singular or plural) must be reformed or refounded and not simply restored to a semblance of former glory. Where are the indications that the Holy Spirit, in our time as in every age, is trying to make all things new, to renew the face of the earth? Should we not be awake and alert to the Spirit's creative disturbance of the *status quo*? Should we not ready ourselves for a New Pentecost, stand up and be counted, nail our colors to the mast, and seek to be led forward by the life-giving Spirit? Our common Christian tradition assures us that God will *never* break the Covenant, Jesus will *never* leave us orphans, and the Spirit will not cease to be committed to *making all things new*. The challenge for all of us Christians is to remain faithful to God and to seek to discern and respond to the Spirit's promptings.

"I BELIEVE IN THE HOLY SPIRIT"

Some people seem to seek the Holy Spirit in a very active way. They know they can never capture, much less domesticate or tame, God's Spirit, but they hope to be captivated and amazed *by* the Paraclete. Others are less active, associating the Spirit with fire or wind or even with a kindly dove, and waiting to be warmed or caressed, comforted or consoled.

In a more general sense, the English language can refer to a person *of spirit*, a team-spirit, a *spirited* performance, a *spirit* of inquiry or solidarity or adventure, even of a broken-*spirited* person: all these uses have connotations of vitality, *creativity*, and *life-force*. Explicitly or implicitly, to talk of spirit is to speak the language of transcendence; it's interesting to note that even in our very materialistic age the idea of spirit has not entirely vanished.

But isn't this use of language simply metaphorical? Or can we claim that the *actual Spirit of God*, the one we call Holy, is really active in the world? Does God's Spirit *inspire* or *animate* us, or any institutions that we know? Do *we* believe that Jesus did not leave us without granting us the *very Spirit of God* to dwell *within* and *among* us, to keep renewing creation, including ourselves?

Practically speaking, it's difficult to think that that many of us actively do believe in this Spirit. It's not so much that we disbelieve, it is that we don't *actively* believe. Few of us show signs of truly believing that the Holy Spirit can be part of any group, and can lead and guide and make holy, and change minds and hearts. If we truly believed that *the Spirit of God* was working in *us* like fire, there would be such commotion in our daily lives that the media would be full of it, and celebrations of Thanksgiving or the Fourth of July would pale by comparison.

There was a moment, once, when those early Christians really shook the world. Is that moment forever past, or can today's believers still generate a similar passion; do some of us still hope fiercely when we say: "We believe in the Holy Spirit, the Lord and Giver of Life, who has spoken through the prophets"?

Lord and Giver of Life? Do those words include life for people in penitentiaries, executed by governors or presidents claiming to be born-again Christians? Is the Spirit *Giver of Life* to "enemy" civilians obliterated in war by order of a commander in chief? Do we believe God's Spirit is *Giver of Life* to the not-yet born and the not-quite dead, about whom legislators presume to pass life-and-death laws?[18] These questions are disturbing to many people: perhaps the Spirit of God is *trying* to disturb us.

What about a Spirit *who has spoken through the prophets?* Are these just long-dead people from another time and place or are they living witnesses: people who speak today and live close by? What difference would it make if we believed in the Spirit of God—a Spirit of life that was speaking through living people, one that was active in our own lives and experience? It would make *a world of difference*. Literally. Latin American liberation theologian José Comblin recently said: "My hope is in the Holy Spirit; I think the third millennium will be the era of the Spirit. The Holy Spirit is very active now, but there is increasing conflict between the churches *as institutions*, and the presence of the Spirit *in people*."[19]

SIGNS OF THE SPIRIT AMONG US

Because *we* organize and control, because *we* decide and make plans, we may not have time to order our lives as if God's Spirit rather than our own intuitions and determinations were leading us. Here are five signs that seem to mark those who really believe in the Spirit of God. They may be worth a little reflection. Such people

- Actually go looking for trouble, for troubled people, as Jesus did;
- Pray to become aware, *to be disturbed*, lest they fail to hear and respond to the cries of the needy and the structures of sin;
- Are united though diverse, so that the world may believe (Jn 17:21);
- Are convinced they can help change the world—or that they will be found guilty if they fail to do so;
- Live exciting and worthwhile lives.

Two thousand years is not long, geologically speaking. But it's an awful long time to wait for the message of Jesus to overcome the world and to convince the poor that God loves them. Even after two millennia, the mistakes, injustices, and sins of baptized Christians and the institutional churches sometimes come close to overwhelming us. For all the Dorothy Days or Mother Teresas, the Dietrich Bonhoeffers or Martin Luther Kings Jr., the Ita Fords or Dorothy Kazels, the Desmond Tutus or Nelson Mandelas, the Oscar Romeros or Joseph Bernardins, there are still many "believers" who seem neither inspired by the Spirit of God nor able or willing to inspire anyone else in God's name. Why are these believers so ambivalent? Here is a handful of possible reasons. They are only suggestions, but they too may merit a moment's consideration. Could it be perhaps, that

- We expect God to work miracles and solve all our problems, so we do nothing—and then complain of the mess;
- We have not looked for God's presence in our daily experience, so the Holy Spirit really does seem invisible;
- We have not allowed our carefully laid plans to be interrupted by the Spirit who wants to *renew the face of the earth* and *make all things new*, including ourselves;
- We have effectively forgotten the Pentecost story, becoming weary or dispirited; and finally,
- We are afraid of what might happen to us if God's Spirit were really fire and wind, a spirit of adventure and risk in our overcautious and controlled lives?

Every year, in every season, we experience the elemental power of nature, in floods and forest fires, in tornadoes and volcanoes, in heat waves and freezing rain. What could we *not* expect if we let the elemental power of the Spirit of the Creator shake the world—and ourselves with it?

The Spirit As Renewer
of the Face of the Earth

The Spirit's job description must include instigating creative interruptions: after all, the *ru'ach* or breath of God that became a figure for the Holy Spirit was brooding over the chaos in the beginning and taking responsibility for creation, a process that changes things. Traditionally, we have prayed to the Holy Spirit to come and "renew the face of the earth." How *on earth* can that happen without some disturbance of what is going on in our own lives? The challenge for us is to allow our lives to be interrupted. But that is easier said than done: as surely as our instinct pulls our hand away from a hot stove, so do we react against whatever interferes with our plans or patterned lives. So what do we do? Either we seek to be led by the Spirit or we resist the Spirit. But we cannot claim to be Spirit-led if our lives are governed and controlled by personal plans and structures. Some of the most gifted of us are the most rigid, making a virtue of being in control and leaving very little room for divine disturbances. Our good and even our best intentions are not enough. All Christian believers are charged to invoke the spirit of their common baptism and to live with greater faithfulness to their call. We need to encourage and support one another in being more generous and committed to the Gospel and in being increasingly responsive to the promptings of the Spirit. Even as we do so, we will perhaps discover that some of our greatest fears will be awakened and that we will be tested beyond our levels of comfort. We have to hold on to the reassurance of Jesus: "Take courage; I have conquered the world" (Jn 16:33).

THE SPIRIT AS DISTURBER

It may be possible to identify some of the ways the Spirit tries to disturb us, and some of the responses or reactions that occur. Then we can more easily gauge how our attitudes need to change if we are to be open to the Spirit. It might be argued that the Spirit is trying to break through and speak to us in all manner of people and situations but that humanity—and the institutional church—is blocking, or muzzling, the Spirit (we will look more closely at this word "muzzle" on page 38).

The Bible is quite clear: we are all made in God's very image: male and female God created humankind; not simply *Adam, the male,* but *Adam'a, the earth person* (Gen 1:27). *Each* is a reflection of God; *both* are constitutive of *humankind. There is no hierarchy.* But—and we will note this on a number of other occasions because of its enormous importance—what God joined together in the beginning, man (in this case *male, cultural* man) quickly divided. Patriarchy creates hierarchy, enthrones males, demeans females, and ultimately fashions a theology that claims this division was actually God's idea. It is not; and the Holy Spirit has been trying to interrupt and undermine these cultural constructs for centuries. The following seven sections detail ways in which the Spirit interrupts human agendas.

The Spirit Disturbs Through Jesus

Jesus proclaimed that men are *not* superior and women are *not* inferior. When his own religious culture claimed that hierarchy was actually part of the Divine plan, Jesus unmasked the lie:[20] in the Jesus society the first must be last, the master must become a servant, and the poor and forgotten "little ones" will be first into God's Realm. This exchange of places is not just a reversal of hierarchy so that women now control men. Nor is it a takeover by women: that would be as sinful as patriarchy. Rather it is a social and religious revolution in which permanent or structural hierarchy is dethroned altogether and a new model of society is advocated.

Not everyone could tolerate this disturbing talk from Jesus. Yet early Christianity had so much promise! Paul insisted that what culture could not do, baptism *in the Spirit of Jesus* could do: create a community of equals. Baptism would not totally erase the dividing lines created by culture, lines of privilege, discrimination and sin; but *in Christ,* sexual and social differences would have no *moral* significance: for in Christ there is no moral distinction between people (Gal 3:28). That is why true Christianity—in the Spirit of Jesus—will always be countercultural, a challenge to every culture, never satisfied with hearing or repeating the cultural sins of sexism, hierarchy, or discrimination. True Christianity will always be a challenge, even and especially to baptized Christians and church structures, because we are all tainted with a spirit of self-interest and discrimination: but that never has been the Holy Spirit of God.

There was a brief moment when Christian males seemed to act in a truly godly way, actually abandoning circumcision, the Jewish sign of exclusiveness and election. In principle, all males— gentile as well as Jew—could now be included in the new community. They were daring and courageous in suggesting that circumcision might have become an ungodly sign of discrimination. It is too bad they lacked the courage to abandon that other critical sign of discrimination: gender; and it is utterly tragic that they kept sexual hierarchy in place, despite the radical equality preached and practiced by Jesus.

The Spirit *tried* to interrupt this male monologue; but a Spirit audible in the silence will be drowned by trumpet blasts and is always ineffective among the willfully deaf. Jesus was constantly appealing to "those who have ears" in his culture; to have the capacity to listen and to hear, in other words "to have ears," was a defining characteristic of a human being. Yet, as he pointed out, not all those with ears act as humans, and not all who claim to be human are prepared to listen.

Will we allow the Spirit to disturb our lives and even lead us into trouble? Or are we looking for the quiet life? "Do not think that I have come to bring peace to the earth; I have not come to bring peace, but a sword" said Matthew's Jesus (Mt 10:34). Luke's Jesus brings a baptism of fire, adding: "How I wish it were already kindled!" (Lk 12:49). Jesus promises anything but the quiet life! Even his peace is quite beyond the world's comprehension: the world simply cannot give it; and the peace that Christ gives resides at the deepest level of one's being, well beneath the surface turbulence. Such peace makes absolutely no sense to those looking for the quiet life. But to those who seek first God's Kingdom or Realm, "these things"—abiding peace and an experience of God's presence—will be added. So the question is: will we let the Spirit lead us into and through political and religious trouble in our troubled world and church?

Jesus was an instrument of the Spirit for disturbing lives, but there are other signs of the Spirit working in and through this world and its people.

The Spirit Disturbs Through Women

Women have always been the life and soul of community, including ecclesial or parish communities. That was true during the life of Jesus and it remained true at his death. Not only did women remain faithful at the Cross, they were the first to witness and proclaim the Resurrection: among the very first *martyrs* and *missionaries*. The early church made a concerted effort to take women seriously, and many women were at the very heart of these communities. As liturgical theologian Gary Macy[21] has shown, the interpretation of medieval liturgies can be extremely problematical, yet he has documented cases of medieval "ordinations" of women. Systematician John Wijngaards claims that in some cases the laying of hands on women followed exactly the same procedure as for men.[22] In any event, it took a good deal more than a millennium to marginalize women permanently and to develop an imperial, patriarchal church.

A recent declaration from Rome asserts that women *cannot* become sacramental ministers and that the church simply *cannot* change this circumstance because it is God's will.[23] However, the issue remains alive and contentious, not least because other Christian denominations have reached very different conclusions on this matter.

A characteristic human flaw is the inability to think one's thinking is wrong; and a typical failure of many Christians is the failure to grasp the revealed truth: that God's image *is* male and female, and that in Christ there is no longer Jew nor Greek, slave nor free, male or female, but all are one. One particularly sad masculine attitude is to declare, to shout, or to halt discussion in an attempt to change reality itself. This effort is rather like an illusionist trying to persuade us that the Statue of Liberty has actually disappeared; we *know* it's not true, even though we can't explain why and, though for a moment, it does appear to have vanished.

So the questions will not simply disappear: is it the Church of Jesus Christ that cannot change or has the thinking of some prelates become limited? Should we conclude that the Spirit is absent from churches that have been ordaining women for half a century? Where is the Spirit who was invoked for a thousand years every time the bishop's hand was laid on women's heads? Jurgen Moltmann, one of the most respected contemporary theologians, says frankly that the patriarchal sins against women are sins against the Holy Spirit.[24] A recent article[25] argues that "there is a serious risk that the church will lose women in this new century the way it lost European working-class men in the last." And if the women have not all left yet, many of their daughters and granddaughters will not be so long-suffering: a huge number have walked away already. Is the Spirit trying to tell us something? The questions are not easy to articulate, nor are the answers easy to be certain of. But an overriding question remains: is the Spirit trying to disturb current thinking about women, about ministry, and about the Church?

The Spirit Disturbs Through Service

The Latin-derived word "magisterium" refers to the teaching authority of the church, understood by Roman Catholics to be exercised by the pope under certain conditions, and collegially by the universal college of bishops. The root of the word "magisterium" means *big;* magisterial describes someone or something authoritative or masterful; its primary reference is to a VIP—a "very important person."[26] The concept of magisterium is at the heart of today's ecclesial structure.

The root of the word "ministerium" means *little.* Ministry refers to attentive service, often inconsequential and almost unnoticed. The word "ministerial" describes someone or something not very important; its primary reference is to a "little person" or a "nobody." The concept of ministry is at the heart of the life of Jesus.

"You must not allow yourselves to be called Master," said Jesus; "you are all brothers and sisters. The greatest must be the servant. If you exalt yourself you *will be* humbled" (paraphrase of Mt 23:8–12). Equality is typical of the early development of small groups. In the earliest days of Christianity, people were explicitly committed to living as equals *under the Spirit* (Acts 2:44). But this model has been increasingly overlooked in twenty centuries of subsequent history, except, of course, by reform movements, many of which have been condemned for their effrontery. Many Christian denominations are explicitly hierarchical, and the effect of their hierarchical structures can be to drive a wedge into the heart of the people of God. Many churchmen take inflated titles[27] such as "Holiness," "Eminence," "Lord," "Monsignor," "Father"—titles expressly forbidden to Matthew's community. Can we notice the Holy Spirit trying to disturb such self-importance in Chapter 23 of Matthew's Gospel—or is that part of the reason why we so rarely mention it?

In some of the Christian churches today, and most obviously in the Roman Catholic church, the magisterial element appears more prominent than the ministerial. Many who are outsiders to institutionalized Christianity are deterred and offended by the pomp and circumstance. At the 1998 Asian Synod of Roman Catholic bishops, a bishop from the Philippines begged the magisterium to pay much more attention to the ministerium of the laity. "Did they ever stop to think," he asked his fellow bishops, "that distrust of the laity might also be distrust of the Holy Spirit?"[28] Only when we have this kind of perception will we notice how quickly we may stifle the Spirit, and how resistant we are to the Spirit's attempts to interrupt our agendas and creatively disturb us.

The Spirit Disturbs Through Ecumenism

Jesus said some very serious things immediately before his Passion. We might think his followers would pay unique and abiding attention to the very last statement attributed to him by John's Gospel: "I ask…that they may all be one. As you, Father, are in me and I am in you, may they also be in us, *so that the world may believe that you have sent me*" [italics added] (Jn 17:21). Paul also asserted that "*in one Spirit* we were all baptized into one body" (1 Cor 12:13).

But we are *not* one. Over two thousand years the Body of Christ has been divided into more than 33,000 fragments or groups claiming to be believers.[29] On the whole, the world does *not* believe that Jesus is the One sent by God. Given the scandalous fragmentation of Christ's body, that result is hardly surprising. We perpetuate historic divisions between the different communities that call on the same Christ. Despite recent Lutheran-Roman agreements on justification by faith—acknowledging five centuries of mutual misunderstandings and the achievement of substantial unity today—still Rome balks. Roman Catholics are told they *cannot* gather at the same table, even with brothers and sisters who believe as passionately as they themselves in the reality of Christ's body and blood. Christians are united in one faith yet divided by one Eucharist. Truly, dialogue and hierarchy are incompatible: they can only alternate or one will inevitably come to dominate the other. Nevertheless, we must never abandon hope because the Holy Spirit continues to seek the conversion of us all. We must be committed to pursuing the elusive unity for which Christ himself prayed and to allowing ourselves to be disturbed by the scandal of a divided Church.

The Spirit Disturbs Through Eucharist

Jesus did not demand that everyone agree with him before they gathered at table. Jesus never assumed that only friends should gather to break bread. Jesus knew that not only do you gather with friends but that unless you gather with enemies or strangers you will never become friends. Jesus knew that you don't only eat with those you agree with or approve of but that eating is a gesture of trust and respect, without which you will never come to agree with or approve of anyone beyond your own narrow, biased circle.

Jesus used meals as a way to encounter and embrace, to teach and reconcile, to heal and unite. He issued and accepted invitations so as to create and foster a *spirit* of reconciliation. He promoted table-fellowship so as to share not only food but the very *Spirit of God* who changes and transforms hearts and lives. Once, when the hungry and *dispirited* disciples asked for some relief for themselves and the crowd, he turned and said: *"You* give them something to eat" [italics added] (Mt 14:16). The pastoral situation today is critical. Disciples must take some initiatives, and the example of Jesus should serve to remind us that God will not intervene where solutions are available and disciples are Spirit-filled. Miracles do not make faith: faith makes miracles.[30] But are we capable of thinking differently? Are we capable of retaining enduring faith in the Spirit? Will we ever allow our well-crafted and time-tabled agendas to be disturbed?

Unity and Eucharist are, of course, interconnected. The Spirit who renews the earth is the Spirit of unity. That same Spirit is at the heart of the food-sharing ministry of Jesus. But what are *we* doing, two thousand years on? We separate and exclude where Jesus gathered and included; we continue to divide what Jesus joined together. Will we ever be open to the inspiration of the Spirit who calls and gathers us, unified but not uniform, united yet diverse? Sometimes people must act on impulse and not wait for an invitation, come for nourishment at the table rather than be taught the niceties of etiquette, choose life and not wait until they become so weakened that they die. Starving people have an absolute right to nourishment: it is a matter of simple justice.

Perhaps in our day as never before, ecumenism and Eucharist offer committed Christians of whatever denominational tradition an opportunity and a challenge to respond to the Spirit in a bold new way, to plead their case, to gather faithfully at the table of the Lord and to keep the memory of Jesus alive. The issue is not subject to simple remedies; but where people of good will gather, the assistance of the Holy Spirit has been promised. Our good will, however, is measured by our willingness to be disturbed by God's Spirit and by our persevering commitment to being converted.

The Spirit Disturbs Through Children

Child-abandonment was institutionalized in the Roman Empire: a citizen who was also a father could choose to ignore or repudiate his own offspring, and the child would then become a legally abandoned nonentity, a nonbeing. The kindness of strangers[31] was then the only hope for such children, and the Church, to its everlasting credit, became strongly committed to rescuing abandoned children and establishing bonds of trust and moral support.

Some of the cruder forms of child-neglect have disappeared, but globally children continue to be abused, abandoned, and deprived on a scale that is truly scandalous. Now, however, it is not only the Roman *paterfamilias*[32] who must take responsibility. Now even some professing Christians—as well as some vowed religious, and clergy—have been exposed as guilty of such neglect and abuse of children. Jesus said some chilling words about this kind of scandal (Mt 18:6).

In the face of abuse and its cover-up, how will we convince people that the Spirit of God is still active in the God's Church rather than compromised by its membership? Psalm 8 proclaims that "out of the mouths of babes" will come praise and acknowl-edgment of God. It is happening. Despite the tendency not to take "babes" seriously (the word "infant" means literally *with-out speech*, and metaphorically it means *having nothing to say*), in the past few years "babes" have been speaking loud and clear about neglect and abuse and betrayal. The Spirit is uncovering some shameful behavior; and if our ecclesial or local response is to deny it—or worse, to try to protect perpetrators and to re-victimize victims—how can we claim to be responsive to the Spirit? The truth is painful; but the Spirit of truth is in the air (and the wind and the stillness), and those who have ears are beginning to hear and to respond. Where there has been some systemic re-sponse, and true concern for victims, there people are being moved by the Spirit of God, the *Advocate* of victims.

The Roman Catholic church proclaims the sanctity of life from conception onward; therefore, it simply cannot look on while systemic poverty and abuse compromise the lives of millions of children. *Each day* some 40,000 children die of starvation. How is the Spirit trying to disturb those who speak of the sanctity of all life? How are we called to become more responsible for one an-other, especially for our most needy and vulnerable? What is God's Spirit trying to tell us as we consider the plight of children in today's world? Earnest declarations about the sanctity of life ring hollow unless they are backed by a consistent ethic and a firm and explicit advocacy on behalf of *all* endangered human lives.

The Spirit Disturbs Through the Poor

Last in our litany of current global challenges: the poor are the fastest-growing population on earth. The number of human be-ings alive today who are either abjectly, desperately, cripplingly poor—or who struggle every single day of their lives for food and survival—is greater than the number of people like us who eat when we're hungry and drink when we're thirsty. Out of every hundred people on earth now, seventeen will die of starvation, a similar number will be permanently impaired—from their brains to their reproductive organs—and another seventeen or so will be forced to beg, steal, or suffer the kind of hunger we cannot imagine. That's more than half the people on earth. Shall we simply say "God help them"?

A thousand years ago, the known world was called *Christendom* and dedicated to Christ. If the potential of early Christianity had been realized, if people had truly been disciples of Christ, is it conceivable that after two thousand years there could be such a catalog of disasters as this? And in the face of all the unfulfilled potential of Christianity and Christians, how can we *not* conclude that we have failed to notice the promptings of the Holy Spirit whose desire and design is to renew the face of the earth and every person of good will? Either the Holy Spirit is a figment of our collective imaginations or something is tying the Spirit's hands, clipping her wings, or acting as a muzzle. If we are serious when we say we believe in the Holy Spirit then we must accept our collective responsibility for disregarding or hobbling God's Spirit. Is this the sin that cannot be forgiven, the sin against the Holy Spirit, about which Jesus spoke enigmatically? (Mt 12:31; Mk 3:28; Lk 12:10).

MUZZLING THE SPIRIT

In recent years people have spoken of the danger of "muzzling the Spirit." What does this mean? We may recall the image of the Suffering Servant in the prophet Isaiah, the servant who "a dimly burning wick he will not *quench*" [italics added] (Isa 42:3). Yahweh is God of nurturing and life, not of destruction and death. Or note the dying words of Stephen: "You stubborn people...*always resisting the Holy Spirit*" (Acts 7:51). Here's the difference between God's ways and ours: God fans the flame, we quench it or smother it; God sustains, we resist or muzzle.

The Letter to the Ephesians urges believers: "Do not grieve the Holy Spirit of God, with which you were marked with a seal for the day of redemption (Eph 4:30). Saint Paul explicitly coached Timothy to *"rekindle the gift of God* that is within you through the laying on of my hands; for God did not give us *a spirit of cowardice* but *rather a spirit power"* (2 Tim 1:6). Even when Paul is in chains, he asserts triumphantly, "[but] the word of God is not chained" (2 Tim 2:9). Yet he also accused the Thessalonians of trying to suppress the Spirit's work. "Do not quench the Spirit," he warns (1 Thess 5:19), implying, of course, that they just might try exactly that.

My characterization of *muzzling* the Spirit can be found in Scripture. The reference to not *muzzling* the ox that treads the grain (Dt 25:4) is reapplied in 1 Corinthians 9:9; 1 Timothy 5:18. By extension, the verbs for *quench, resist, suppress,* and *chain up* serve to identify processes that stifle or restrain. Stephen goes to his death warning of such resistance to the Holy Spirit. In our turn, we must not oppose God's Spirit, must not extinguish the flame of Pentecost ignited so long ago. Yet we must be aware that *it is always possible* to quench that flame or muzzle the Spirit; God forces no one, and sometimes we act contrary to God's designs. Therefore we *must ask* if we are guilty of sinning against the Spirit in this way.

The ox that turns the grindstone to mill flour may be muzzled (though the Bible expressly forbids this in Deuteronomy 25:4: let the animal eat and survive, for God's sake). You may muzzle a pig because pigs are rooters: they disturb the land, looking for food and turning a field upside down. A dog that bites, or even barks or frightens someone, may need to be muzzled. And you should muzzle a potentially rabid animal so that you don't catch something nasty. In short, you muzzle powerful, disturbing, or hungry animals, or those you can't control. You don't muzzle cats or donkeys: they are predictable and not likely to surprise you. People muzzle what is *stronger than* they feel they can otherwise cope with.

How can we apply this to the Holy Spirit? God's Spirit *wants* to share our food and disturb our garden, to bark and surprise us, even to light a few fires, to speak words that are unpopular to some, to disturb the peace of others, or to make people uncomfortable. But if the Spirit can be muzzled, life goes on in the same placid way; and people remain comfortable, undisturbed, and unaware: they hear nothing. And that's exactly why Saint Paul urges believers *not* to muzzle or quench, or resist, or suppress God's Spirit: *the Spirit's job is to make a commotion,* to sound

the alarm, to surprise people, and to galvanize disciples as part-
ners in changing the world. The Spirit's mission is nothing less
than to *renew the face of the earth.* The Spirit is not a spirit of
domesticity like a pussy cat nor a docile beast of burden like a
donkey.

Chaos and Creativity

Since the beginning, the Spirit has been *part of the chaos,* attend-
ing to the unfinished business of creation, defending the needs of
the world, opposing the vandalism and destruction of demented
humanity. The Spirit is *trying* to interrupt us—individually and
as congregations—precisely when we refuse to be shocked and
galvanized into action, even as we resist the cries of the poor,
blame the victims, and justify our own comforts and achievements.

Occasionally, some of us are aware of the chaos and of how
close it comes to swirling all round us. Some of us are outraged
by the injustice that maintains it. And we—by profession of our
belief in Christ—should be deeply committed to looking into the
faces of the actual flesh-and-blood victims scattered around our
cities and our world like global trash or international garbage.
The marginalized poor, homeless women and men who live on
the streets, runaway kids, addicts of all ages; people out of work,
on welfare, in or out of prison; the mentally ill, the old and physically weak; outsiders, strangers, immigrants, foreigners; people
we don't like or just don't get along with. All these, we claim to
believe, are as cherished by God as any of us. Each one is as much
a human person as we are. But unless we persevere as Jesus did
and continue to be involved, we are not yet worthy to be called
Christians because we are not led by the Spirit who disturbs and
interrupts.

Chaos is potentially good: it is the raw material from which
the Spirit created the cosmos. So if we identify the chaos in the
cosmos today, perhaps we are close to seeing where and how the
Spirit is trying to break through, in order to *renew the earth.* But
do we have the capacity, or the imagination, to be disturbed enough
to respond, when periodically we are interrupted from our com-

placency or our preoccupation with our own good little lives? When the Son of Man separates people like sheep and goats, *everyone* will be surprised (cf Mt 25:35). It is those who were *inspired to be disturbed* and to do something about it by aiding the sick, the imprisoned, the hungry, or the naked, those will be called the righteous. Meanwhile, others failed to notice, shrugged it off, were busy doing other things, did not want to get involved, or simply didn't think. That's the trouble with many of us: we just don't think. That's way the Spirit continues to act as a disturbing presence in our lives: to make us think, to make us act.

This is precisely the glory of the community of *all* those who share the common name of Christian. Each baptized person is called to be the bearer of a common tradition, to be faithful to the memory and the call of Jesus. Many of us have memories of being inspired. Can it happen again? Can we fan the flame so that it burns fiercely once more? Can we help reanimate our communities and congregations, our divided denominations and the one Church to which we are all called—or will the embers lose their heat and will the fire turn to ash?

SUMMARY

This chapter began with the story of Susan Classen and of new life coming from dying plant-cuttings. We looked at the Spirit's power to work through Jesus, through women, through service, through ecumenism, through eucharist, through children, and through the poor. And we asked, rhetorically, if the Spirit's work in these areas was affecting us and our own lives. But the most fundamental question of all is simply this: could any of this make a difference in our lives or the lives of others?

The Holy Spirit, given to us in baptism and long before, renewed in confirmation and long before, is not only the invisible and overlooked member of the Trinity but the one that is least effective in many of our lives. God, Creator or Father, we can handle when we look at a newborn child or witness a blazing sunset. God, Savior or Son, we can relate to in the feeding of the five thousand or the washing of the disciples's feet, or even in the figure on the Cross. But God the Holy Spirit? The Spirit may be subtle, silent, unseen, elusive. But the Spirit is committed to radical transformation and conversion. We are included. We are invited. That's what our baptism *is:* baptism *in and by* the Holy Spirit of God. Our lives and the lives of the very least of the brothers and sisters of Jesus depend on our keeping that baptism alive like an eternal flame. This duty, of course, is a matter of faith: it is an invitation to have our lives disturbed and rearranged, and a blueprint for finding meaning in our lives. Even for those whose faith is as small as a mustard seed, it is *never* too late; we *can respond,* because now is the acceptable time, and because this is the day of salvation (2 Cor 6:2).

CHAPTER THREE

Imagination, Encounter, Ministry

IN THE MOOD FOR MINISTRY

It is important to reiterate that true Christian discipleship is not measured simply by the capacity to be a presence that disturbs others; we must first have felt God's disturbing presence within ourselves. That is what rearranges the contours of our own lives, gives our lives meaning, and motivates us to be concerned about others. We may recall Frankl's axiom (p. xvii) that to love we must encounter: it is our *God-inspired* restlessness that compels us—commissions us—to reach out to encounter. Every authentic faith-driven encounter with another person is a form of ministry. However inconsequential it may seem, it can change the world.

Most people see the world in a rather limited fashion: they see what is or what appears to be rather than what is coming to be or what might be. They live, as it were, locked in the *indicative mood*. Grammatically, a *mood* is the inflection of a verb that expresses its function. Many of us will remember from schooldays learning a foreign language, with the inevitable verbs, regular and irregular, in a variety of *moods* (technically, apart from the infinitive and the indicative, they are the subjunctive, imperative, interrogative and optative; to these we can add the affirmative and negative forms). But unless we became quite proficient in speaking that language, we probably only learned to use the indicative mood, and were therefore restricted to making statements: "I am, you are, he/she/it is, we are, you are, they are." We were able to describe what is, or what appears to be, the case, but not much else, apart from the ability to make our statements negative as well as positive. Perhaps we also managed the easiest of all, the interrogative mood, for as long as we knew the indicative mood, asking questions was often a simple matter of word inversion: "This is a soldier" can become "Is this a soldier?" And so on.

Do the limits of our own language—and the limits of our language skills—also mark the limits of our own lives? Is our whole existence metaphorically limited to the indicative and interrogative moods? Do we simply acknowledge or react to what *is* ("I am in a rut"; "You are my enemy"; "He is a fool"; "She is my best friend") or what *is not* ("It is not raining"; "We are not talking to each other"; "They are not friendly") without thinking of the possibility of changing ourselves, our relationships, and maybe even the world? Or do our lives at least include lots of questions (the interrogative mood), though not with any real hopes of their generating answers? Perhaps we interrogate ourselves wistfully: "Am I the only one who thinks this way?"; "Am I happy?"; "Do I really believe?" and so on. But do we *seriously* look for answers? Are even our own questions merely rhetorical? And as we look around, do we get the impression that many of our contemporaries are going through the same motions, vaguely looking for meaning, intermittently searching for answers—or living no better than one-dimensional and rather flat lives? Are there, then, any alternatives, for ourselves or for others?

Let us exploit the ambiguity of this word "mood." Grammatically, it expresses changes in the form of the verb, corresponding to a speaker's feeling or capacity. In a different context, we also speak of *moods* to refer to aspects of temperament or displays of emotion. Just as the use of various grammatical moods extends our control over a language, so a range of emotional moods can express different possibilities and approaches to life.

Some people live rather blandly, limited to in the *indicative mood*. Their experience of life is reduced to what actually is. But active agents, rather than simply observers or pawns, discover how to live more richly and ask what *might be* or what *could be*. Instead of settling for what is, we might become more active and employ the *interrogative*, asking *what if?* or *why not?* These questions raise serious possibilities: with them, we might even be able to change the world. A thought experiment may allow us the luxury of imagining how our lives, like our speech, might be enriched if we could operate with greater flexibility.[33]

The *subjunctive mood* indicates possibility or supposition, hypothesis or doubt. Sentences such as "*If I were* ten years younger...*"; "*I would* like to be...*"; or "*It could be* a lot better/ worse*" are constructed in the subjunctive mood. They allow for a range of expressions, not simply of what is, but of what might be and of what can be imagined: "*If you want* to be my disciple...*" is formulated in the subjunctive. What if our lives were constructed on similar premises? Indeed, the phrase "what if...?" is not only in the subjunctive mood but also in the interrogative. Perhaps our lives could reflect similar *moods*, or subtleties. *If* we want to make a difference, *then* we have to change the way we live. What *if* we were to think differently about our faith, and then to act differently?

The *optative mood* handles wishes and dreams, preferences and choices. In poetic form, this mood may be indicated by the word "O," as in "O for the wings of a dove!" or "O that I might do great things." But this mood also indicates wishes that are not simply vain but which are filled with hope: "*I wish* I could help," or "*I would love* to be more faithful to the Gospel." How might the focus and effectiveness of our lives be sharpened and improved if we were to develop the optative possibilities (like a waking dream or creative imagining of what is not but might still be). This premise is not wishful thinking, but a real prayer or invocation: "O that I had the courage of my convictions!" "O that I were more open to God's transforming power, rather than content to stay in the rut!" South African Missiologist David Bosch once described a rut as a shallow grave.

The *imperative* mood gets things moving, but usually by means of others: "*Come*, follow me"; "*Go*, and sin no more!"; "*Stretch out* your hand!"; "*Be* cured!" But it is also capable of galvanizing a community: "*Let us* do something"; "Give them something to eat yourselves"; "Gather up the fragments"; or even "Lord, *teach* us to pray!" The imperative can change the world. If our lives were more intentionally affected by the imperative, we might change the world too: "*Let me* volunteer!"; "*Let us* do justice!"

The *interrogative mood* is capable of creating relationships, for the act of asking questions indicates a relationship with someone outside ourselves. Jesus said that we should ask, but people who do not seek relationships or who think they know the answers do not ask. The interrogative can say, "*May I* be of assistance?"; "*What* do you want me to do for you?"; "*Why* do you call me good?"; "*Will you* also go away?"; "*Can* my sons sit at your right hand?" Perhaps if there were more of an interrogative mood in our lives there would be more interaction, more involvement, and more avenues to explore. But those who do not ask are less likely to receive and more likely to remain as they were. Perhaps that is why we don't ask.

Our lives are often drab and uninspiring because our imaginations are not stimulated and because we seem content to react to what is rather than to look at what might be. It may be time for a mood swing, away from the limitations of living in the indicative. To ask *Why not?* and to imagine *What if?* is to be more interrogative, more questioning and more open to learning. It also extends our range, spiritual as well as grammatical.

We can push our thought experiment further: it is often possible to choose between *affirmative* and *negative* formulations, and sometimes we can become very attached to the negative: "I don't like the way we do liturgy"; "You can't say that"; "He/she/it won't work in *this* parish"; "Let us not even *think* of that"; "People won't like it." We have probably all heard this kind of *negative* statement and we do not need to dwell upon it here. But how different if we really tried to use the *affirmative* style: "I will be glad to help"; "You are doing a wonderful job"; "He/she/it is very welcome"; "We can make it work"; "They are a real credit to this parish." The Christian community should be marked by affirmation and committed to eradicating a spirit of negativity. As the Letter to the Ephesians has it: "Put away from you all bitterness and wrath and anger and wrangling and slander, together with all malice, and be kind to one another, tenderhearted, forgiving one another, as God in Christ has forgiven you" (Eph 4:31–32).

IMAGINATION, MEANING-MAKING, AND FAITH

People whose lives are governed by the theological virtues of faith, hope, and love are called to live beyond what simply is. After all, faith is a commitment beyond our limited understanding and beyond the convenience of empirical evidence; hope is unshakable confidence in promises that remain valid beyond today; and love is an experience of God beyond ordinary human experience: it is an experience touched by the mystical. Theologian Reinhold Niebuhr once said, "Nothing worth doing is completed in our lifetime. Therefore we must be saved by hope." But if we are to live beyond what actually is, without living in cloud-cuckoo-land, we have to be able to identify the gap between what is and what is yet to be or what might be, and then discover how to survive there.

The Korean Presbyterian theologian Jung Young Lee has written about people who live "in between" different worlds, or "in both" or "in neither," as well as about those who are able to live "in beyond."[34] Today's radical Christian, disturbed by God, must choose to live "in beyond," to bridge the gap between what is and what ought to be. Not that this living on the edge or at the margins is comfortable; it is not. Nor is it predictable or easy to control. But it is life-giving for those with imagination.

The dictionary is often the refuge of tired minds, but it *is* enlightening to look at definitions of the word "imagination." Here are some, with emphasis marked:

- the faculty of imagining: of forming mental images or concepts of *what is not actually present* to the senses, or of *what has not been experienced;*

- mental creative ability;
- *capacity to face and resolve difficulties; resourcefulness;*
- *ability* to deal resourcefully with *unexpected or unusual problems* or circumstances;
- *power of recombining former experiences* in the creation of *new images directed at a specific goal, or aiding in the solution of problems.*

Here are several notions that are potentially very productive for anyone trying to live creative discipleship in a changing world. Creativity is one aspect of the Holy Spirit's commitment to making all things new, to renewing the face of the earth. This statement implies, to use different words, that the endpoint—the *terminus ad quem*—toward which things are tending is actually something new and not simply an extension of the way things currently are. It also implies that imagination is one of the key qualities of those who are working in situations of change or in situations where the future is not predictable. If we are to be led by the Holy Spirit or if we are to look creatively to find where the Holy Spirit might actually be working, then we need imagination. Without it we will be imprisoned in the indicative way of thinking; with it we will be able to ask *What if?* and *Why not?*

Imagination, as the definitions given previously indicate, is the activation of a capacity to cope with what has not actually happened before. It requires creative adaptation and the power to call on past experience and apply it to unfolding events. Since resourcefulness is a necessary component of imagination, one needs to have access to resources accumulated over a period of time. Imagination is thus a quality that can develop through exposure to, and reflection on, a variety of challenges and problems. Moreover, imagination thrives in contexts marked by the unexpected or unusual—provided, of course, that the imaginative person perceives such contexts as potentially enriching rather than simply as bewilderingly new.

In another context we also commonly think of imagination as a characteristic of young children. Perhaps this association is something Jesus was endorsing when he asserted that children would be first in the realm of God: they have the imagination, the adaptability, the natural resourcefulness of those for whom life is adventure rather than either problem or repetition. Some children seem to have a wonderful imagination, only to have it knocked out of them at home or at school; they grow up to be timid and overcautious adults. Some families and communities simply cannot cope with too much imagination.

If we stop to look around, to think of the place of imagination in our lives, and to count the imaginative people we know, there may be lessons to learn. Assuming our imaginations are stimulated and we have imaginative friends, we probably lead exciting lives, full of creative possibilities. Statistically, however, it is more likely that we find our imaginations inhibited rather than stimulated, and that the number of our imaginatively creative friends is small. This result arises from the fact that many of us—whether by temperament or by training—are sensibly conservative and prudent rather than enthusiastic experimenters and risk-takers. But the life of faith and the needs of the people of God require that we balance conservatism and prudence with experiment and risk-taking. This task is not easy, for trial and error necessarily go hand in hand; yet many of us have been taught that we can only undertake the trial when there is absolutely no risk of error or that any error vitiates future trials. Such an attitude produces fearful and stunted adult human beings—the very opposite of what Jesus was seeking.

We are familiar with "think tanks" as virtual laboratories where intelligent people gather to address serious problems. Sometimes they produce wonderful new ideas and technologies—from satellites to moon landers, from videotape to lap-top computers, and from credit cards to fax machines. But sometimes they do not: eight-track tapes and polyester shirts, airline food and asbestos tiles, tea bags and plastic bags, have not been the most significant contributions to civilization. And where think tanks have succeeded best may be where the thinkers were also the most imaginative people. But the two qualities do not always coexist.

What if we were to look for the imaginative people in our workplaces, our communities, and certainly in our worshiping communities? What if we were to encourage "imagination tanks" where imaginative people gather, not to address a particular limited problem, but to imagine a different world—one where people behave differently and different solutions may arise? What if? Why not?

IMAGINATION: THE DYNAMO FOR MINISTRY

As a spur to reflection—imaginative reflection—on the subject of encounter and ministry, here are a dozen statements about the significance of imagination from people who were creative thinkers, who possessed great imagination.

Imagination cannot make fools wise;
but she can make them happy, to the envy of reason,
who can only make her friends miserable.

BLAISE PASCAL (1623–1662)

One of Pascal's famous *pensées*, this statement seems to contain at least a trace of cynicism: imagination can make fools happy. But even that is more than can be said of reason, says Pascal. But do these assertions bear scrutiny? Imagination can make people—and not only fools—happy in the sense that it can afford them the possibility both of conceiving of change and actually undertaking it. The twentieth-century troubadour John Lennon captured the imagination of many with his song "Imagine." Some people who heard it found that it not only lifted their spirits but provided the incentive and possibility for their activism. As to the second assertion, Pascal claims that reason can only make people miserable. Perhaps he means that reason is grounded, whereas imagination can take wing; that reason is able to analyze what actually is, here and now, but is powerless to address other possibilities or to ask *Why not?*

> *Reporting facts is the refuge of those*
> *who have no imagination.*
> MARQUIS DE VAUVENARGUES (1715–1747)

Again, facts are statements of what is: they belong in the indicative mood. Hopes are those things imagined but not yet realized. Those who *only* "report facts" or who are constrained by what actually is, may have a place to live, but it is more like a refuge than a campground, more of a protected and sheltered place to run away to rather than an open and exposed *pied à terre* from which to encounter new worlds.

> *The greatest instrument of moral*
> *good is the imagination;*
> *and poetry administers to the effect*
> *by acting upon the cause.*
> PERCY BYSSHE SHELLEY (1792–1822)

This statement is a weighty one. To assert that imagination is the *greatest* instrument of moral good is to invite a considered response. Indeed, if we employ our imagination—and if we imagine justice and peace, compassion and reconciliation—then not only do we give ourselves the possibility of doing something rather than simply doing nothing, but the very capacity to imagine has itself contributed to the moral good, both of those whose imagination spurs them to action and of those who benefit from it.

But Shelley's explanation is actually more subtle and creative: imagination is to moral good, as cause is to effect. Poetry acts on the cause (imagination) and thereby contributes to the effect (moral good). Therefore, poetry produces moral good. Again, reflection bears this out: the poetic turn of phrase (and perhaps we could add music and art) can raise the mind above what actually is and inspire us to dream of what does not yet exist; and being assisted to dream dreams and to ask *Why not?* is to be enabled to change the world.

In times when the passions are beginning
to take charge of the conduct of human affairs,
one should pay less attention to what men
of experience and common sense are thinking,
than to what is preoccupying the imagination of dreamers.
ALEXIS DE TOCQUEVILLE (1805–1859)

The author of *Democracy in America* knew something about the subject at hand, and he identifies the same issue as does Pascal: that experience, reason, and common sense can sometime restrict rather than inspire our thinking. "When passions are beginning to take charge of the conduct of human affairs" could refer to many contemporary situations in society, the church, or the world at large—from treatment of homosexual persons, to women's ordination, to capital punishment, to economic sanctions that affect innocent nationals. Plenty of people are using their experience and common sense, yet failing to move beyond what is. Dreamers are not entirely constrained by what is (though daydreamers are quite unrelated to what is). Dreamers may ultimately contribute to new ways of thinking. Without imaginative people, the slave trade would never have been abolished, cigarette smokers would have continued to pollute lives, ecumenical agreements would depend on submission or surrender, and we would not have the Internet. The assertion of de Tocqueville could almost be glossed by the ancient prophecy in the book of Joel: After plagues have ceased and the spirit of God has been poured out, "your sons and your daughters shall prophesy, / your old men shall dream dreams / and your young men shall see visions. / Even on the male and female slaves… / I will pour out my spirit" (Joel 2:28–29).

Put off your imagination as you put off your overcoat,
when you enter the laboratory. But put it on again,
as you put on your overcoat, when you leave.
CLAUDE BERNARD (1813–1878)

There are times when the indicative mood is called for. "The laboratory" here represents the world of precision and attention to what actually is. However, it is important to leave the laboratory from time to time and when we do so to adapt our behavior accordingly. But some people seem to have a "laboratory mentality," and to be incapable of adapting to anything other than a controlled atmosphere. Sometimes they try to control the world itself. Imagination allows us to reflect on complexity and chaos, but does not paralyze us in the face of unforseen or uncontrolled situations. The world, the Christians churches, and the disciples of Christ badly need imagination.

> *Must a Christ perish in every age,*
> *to save those that have no imagination?*
> GEORGE BERNARD SHAW (1856–1950)

This quotation is from Shaw's *St. Joan.* Out of context it could mean different things. For me, its appeal lies in the fact that it charges many or most of us with an impoverished understanding of who and what Christ is. If we had a little more imagination we might be able not simply to comprehend the Gospel or even to believe in the Christ of faith but to actually probe the deeper significance of the Incarnation: Emmanuel—God with us. If we could do that, we could never continue to live blandly day after day, because our lives would indeed be transformed. But as long as our imagination is impoverished, it would take at least a second Incarnation to convince us of God's love in Jesus. Even then, it would be insufficient: we simply would not have the capacity to believe it.

> *Every great advance (in science) has issued*
> *from a new audacity of imagination.*
> JOHN DEWEY (1859–1952)

The American pragmatist philosopher and educator was strongly opposed to the notion that reality is static. For him, everything is subject to change and transformation. Imagination allows us to engage with a changing world and to become forces for change ourselves. The more we experience, the more we can recombine accumulated experiences in order to address the changing circumstances of life. Audacity of imagination is needed as much for the advancement of theology and the promotion of authentic missionary Christianity as it is for scientific developments.

> *Without this playing with fantasy,*
> *no creative work has ever yet come to birth.*
> *The debt we owe to the play of imagination is incalculable.*
> CARL GUSTAV JUNG (1875–1955)

The poet Coleridge distinguished imagination from fancy. Fancy—the power to conceive and represent novel imagery—was, for him, synonymous with fantasy. It was also held to be more casual and superficial than imagination. Imagination then, both for Coleridge and for Jung, appears to be an intentional or active property of the mind: a mental faculty. Jung seems to be arguing here both for a context of freedom or leisure in which to indulge the mind's fullest capacities and for the development of improvable skills without which human creativity is seriously compromised. Many people who are deeply committed to justice and who struggle against oppressive structures are nevertheless overwhelmed by the problems and subject to burnout in ministry. Perhaps a serious attempt to incorporate fantasy (fancy) and imagination into our lives, at the personal level but also at the community level, would offer us less stress-filled and more pastorally rewarding lives.

> *Imagination is more important than knowledge.*
> ALBERT EINSTEIN (1879–1955)

Given the author of this one-liner, and his achievements in both physics and world peace, this *pensée* could surely stand on its own as a topic for meditation.

> *The way the world is imagined determines at any*
> *particular moment what [people] will do.*
> WALTER LIPPMANN (1889–1974)

The U.S. political commentator had a wide exposure to cultures and political systems. His words echo linguists' insights: people become effectively imprisoned in their various worlds if their thoughts and actions are constrained by limitations of religion, language, or ethnicity. It also echoes a saying of Ralph Waldo Emerson: "People see only what they are prepared to see." The exercise of the imagination offers a way of opening up worlds that are otherwise enclosed. Unless we actively develop our imagination, however, it may well atrophy, leaving us caught in our actual worlds and unable to develop creative responses to life's daily challenges.

> *[We must discover] the exquisite balance*
> *between the gravity of knowing and*
> *the abandonment of imagination.*
>
> VIRGINIA TRIOLI

This challenging statement was made during an interview; out of context, it allows for the full play of our own creative thinking. The word "exquisite" here surely means *delicate*. We must indeed maintain the appropriate tension or equilibrium between two poles: a delicate balance. The term "gravity of knowing" could refer to the fact that we have a serious responsibility for the knowledge we possess. Knowledge is not simply accumulated facts (that would be an encyclopedia) but awareness or consciousness of external reality. And since knowledge is embodied or held in earthen vessels, its possession carries with it moral responsibility: this is its "gravity."

On the other hand, the "abandonment of imagination" speaks of adventure in a world that might, yet does not actually, exist at this point in time. Such adventure or mental experiment is certainly not to be taken lightly (it is, as far as we know, a quintessentially human capacity); yet it does not have the "gravity of knowing" nor does it impose moral responsibility. Imagination, however, carries with it enormous potential: it is a fulcrum with which to move the world. To maintain the balance or tension between what is and what might be, between the indicative and the subjunctive mood, between knowledge and imagination, would seem to be a most worthy and noble undertaking.

> *The poetic tradition of exile fills out the future in acts*
> *of buoyant imagination: even in dire times, God is*
> *giving newness. God will stay in the crisis until God has*
> *brought the world right. Jeremiah, Ezechiel, and later*
> *Isaiah are full of prophetic imagination.*
> WALTER BRUEGGEMANN

Our final quotation on the subject of imagination provides us with an explicit faith-context for our thoughts. Brueggemann echoes a thought of Elie Wiesel, Nobel Peace prize winner and Auschwitz survivor, that though God begins things and puts the world in motion, God also gives us the power to begin again and again. This power is not simply the ability to repeat acts indefinitely but to think differently; and that prepares a way to repentance. Brueggemann's insight is that God inspires us to use our imagination and that God is with us in our imaginings. If we trust God, we can be bold and faithful at the same time. The prophets show us the way. We can follow them, not only by walking in their footsteps but by imitating their bold faithfulness.

IMAGINATIVE MINISTRY

The God who disturbs us is the God who shows us how to shake a complacent world and disturb the *status quo:* the way things actually are, though not the way they need be or should be. Relatively few people, however, have the capacity or receive the encouragement to think differently with a view to acting differently. Consequently, some of our best intentions remain just that: a predisposition for action or an orientation of the mind but not a purposeful undertaking that affects other people or the world. The road to hell is paved with such intentions. In our daily experience we need to be able to identify people with imagination. Then, perhaps, we can encourage these imaginative people. Still, some of us appear to be threatened by these very people;

we actually prefer the relative predictability of the status quo. Perhaps in this situation an examination of conscience is indicated.

What kinds of people have imagination? Here is a listing of ten kinds of people or a single idealized person. It is neither scientific nor exhaustive but may stimulate reflection and conversation that perhaps are precursors to action. People with imagination are

- People with wide exposure to life;
- People who are encouraged and supported;
- People who find time, make time, enjoy leisure, and can relax;
- People of meditation, contemplation, and prayer;
- People with a sense of humor and lightness of heart;
- People who can forgive themselves;
- People who are truly interested in other people;
- People who ask, seek, and knock, and are appropriately inquisitive;
- People whose minds and worlds are open to alternatives;
- People who actively exercise their imagination and are not content to accept the way things are.

If there is merit in this list, it is worth noting that people with imagination need to be risk-takers and to be within a community which encourages and supports such risk-taking. Prudence cannot be cast to the winds, yet without the possibility of failure we cannot grow to our human potential. There must always be an element of calculated risk in our lives lest we be limited to the possible and prevented from dreaming the impossible dream— which is surely what being a Christian is supposed to be about. But some noble and generous souls are so inhibited from living daring, heroic lives that they either wither or withdraw from the Christian community. An obsessive church or a frightened community which tries to exclude all possibility of making mistakes is a church set back on its heels or a community that has lost its soul. We must be encouraged to strive for great things, to aspire to self-transcendence, and to never give up, though the path be strewn with the rocks of mistakes and failure: "Take courage," says Jesus. "I have conquered the world!" (Jn 16:33).

Here is a little test that can be self-administered or provide an opportunity for conversation with others, whether in the context of an intentional community, a family, or parish-gathering.

1. Rate yourself for imagination or imaginativeness, on a scale of 1 — 10.
2. Rate other people in the group, and the group itself, on the same scale.
3. Discuss your ratings with the broader group. You may include your self-rating or omit that rating if it better serves the group. But reflect on the significance of that choice.
4. Can you agree on the *most imaginative person* in your group? Is that person actually present? If not, what does that suggest?
5. What is your community's attitude to imagination or imaginative people?
6. Do you favor "think tanks" over "imagination tanks" when serious and long-term decisions have to be made?
7. How do you personally stimulate and encourage imagination: in yourself? in others?
8. Imagine an "imagination tank" for your community. How might it be constituted? What might it address?
9. Estimate some possible reactions within the community itself to the notion of an imagination tank.

In a very well-known book of seventy years ago, historian Arthur Nock averred: "The receptivity of most people for that which is totally new...is small. The originality of a prophet lies commonly in [the prophet's] ability to fuse into a white heat combustible material which is there, to express and appear to meet the half-formed prayers of some at least of [the] contemporaries. The message of John the Baptist and of Jesus, gave form and substance to the dreams of a kingdom which had haunted many of their compatriots for generations."[35] This observation expresses very well the importance of imagination for renewing the life of a community and implicitly reminds us that many, or most, of the members of a community may join in opposition to the prophetic imagination. So it was when Jesus proclaimed the Good News, and so may be for his followers everywhere. Even good news is contextualized: it is not—or it is not perceived as—good news for everyone.

MINISTRY TRANSFORMED: VISION, STRATEGY, STRUCTURE

If we can make the assumption—admittedly significant—that we are not content to live in the indicative mood, to settle for the way things are, but are asking *What if?* or *Why not?*, seeking new possibilities, and knocking on closed doors, how might we hope for life-giving developments in ministry? By examining the relationship between vision, strategy, and structure, we may be able to imagine a way forward.

"Where there is no vision the people perish" (Prov 29:18); or in the Jerusalem Bible translation "where there is no vision, the people get out of hand." Either way, there is no question of the prime importance of a forward-looking vision. That is to say, it is simply preposterous—upside down or back to front—to try to work out strategies before we articulate a vision. Without a vision—and even where there is a structure—the people perish. We might show the relationship between structure, strategy, and vision in this way:[36]

VISION
⬆
STRATEGY
⬆
STRUCTURE

We must always begin with a vision, which Jonathan Swift described as "the art of seeing things invisible." Perhaps an even better definition is the art of *making invisible things visible*. Assuming that there is a vision then, strategy exists to serve and promote the vision, while structure is the existential base from which strategies are determined. Structure identifies the rules and exigencies of our daily lives. It would be as futile to imagine we could start from some place other than where we are, as it would be naive to attempt to create strategies unless we had a vision of what these strategies are to serve. Yet many organizations and movements either presume that the creation of strategies is their first priority or simply lack a sustaining vision.

Not long ago a newspaper reported that Christie Tyler, a fortysomething chief executive, completed fifteen company mergers in a single year. An analyst said: "It's the vision thing. He doesn't sit around thinking about his vision after he formulates it. He is very good strategically. He can think and plan ahead. He has a strong intellectual capacity to develop strategy, and has proven that." When Tyler joined his company three years before, the company's vision was limited to being an accounting and software group; he articulated a new vision.

For Christians, the vision to cling to is the vision of the kingdom or realm of God, about which Jesus says many things and offers many images. It is "like treasure hidden in a field, which someone found and hid; then in his joy he goes and sells all that he has and buys that field"; and again, "the kingdom of heaven is like a merchant in search of fine pearls; on finding one pearl of great value, he went and sold all that he had and bought it" (Mt 13:44–46). It is perfectly clear even from these two compressed images that one must have a vision of the kingdom of heaven (a hidden treasure; a valuable pearl). Then one formulates a strategy [seek, find, sell everything, buy]. But it is equally important to start from one's actual context or structure [the home which one leaves in order to go searching; the store or market, which the merchant calls his base].

In order for the vision to remain in view, the structure must be flexible and adaptable: rigid structures may actually serve to

obscure the vision; and energies devoted to maintaining structures may actually be needed in order to sustain the vision. Sometimes it may be necessary to put some distance between ourselves
and our structures in order to be free to dream.

In preparation for celebrating Jubilee 2000, the buildings of
the Vatican—from foundations to facades and from classical sites
to colossal statues—were renovated at enormous cost. A huge
amount of time, effort, and financial resources was poured into a
structural renovation. Ironically, fourteen years earlier in Australia, Pope John Paul II himself had said that he did not even know
which room [in the papal apartments] was which. He told fourth-
grade children that their [class] rooms were more important to
him than all the rooms in the Vatican.[37] The problem is well-stated:
the structures of the Vatican—actual architectural, security and
diplomatic structures—were *preventing* the pope from knowing
actual people. This particular prisoner of the Vatican has indeed
tried to break out, yet he has also been criticized for encountering
only certain "approved" people. For him, the structure inhibits
the strategy. And that is even more true of the Roman Curia. If
we are caught up in structures, we simply cannot exercise our imagination and promote a vision. But what if...? What if there were
an earthquake in Rome? What if the Vatican apartments and the
Curial offices actually collapsed? Would they simply be rebuilt or
would a glimpse of a vision of the kingdom or realm of God
allow for new strategies—and renewed structures to serve them?

In a reflective comment, David Steindl-Rast, a Benedictine
monk from New Camaldoli in Big Sur, California, reminds us
that institutions are always in competition with one another and
that people are needed to maintain institutions. They support the
current structures. Yet, as he says, "while life creates structures,
structures don't create life. So we have to keep the spirit going,
the life strong, and then we will create the structures we need at a
given time. My counsel...would be 'don't focus so much on the
institution. The institutional structure serves life; it is not life that
serves the structure. So look at the life.' If that life happens to
occur somewhere else—not inside the structure but outside the
structure—then be open to it. And if that life is so strong and so

new that it bursts the existing structure, allow that to happen. The structure will renew itself. Life does that all the time. Every Spring, all the protective structures that are around the little leaves burst and fall off. And in the middle of the new leaves, the structure which will protect next year's growth is already forming. So let it happen. Take seriously that for which you are created as a structure, and that is the life. This is very difficult advice to take, because institutions have a built-in tendency to perpetuate themselves....Structures are potentially dangerous enemies if you alienate them, and potentially helpful allies if you get them on your side."[38]

So there it is: vision, strategy, and structure. The three are interrelated, yet grave dangers lie in wait for those who simply try to maintain structures, those whose strategy is detached from a vision, and indeed those whose vision is no better than wishful thinking. The vision can only be kept alive if there are people willing to live for it and die for it. Even a vision cannot retain its pristine attraction indefinitely but must be carried on shoulders, embodied in people, and sustained by strong hearts. Since the vision does not live simply in the indicative mood but requires a variety of moods for its expression, here is a catalog of imperatives[39] (it could just as easily be a list of interrogatives, or questions to be asked of those who presume to carry a vision). It is imperative, then, that a vision be modified as follows:

1. *Reframed.* It cannot become the reiteration of a tired formula or wish list. A vision must be connected to people's dreams but in new and varied ways. The vision is an image or metaphor of a *tertium quid:* a third thing, a new reality, something unknown, yet related to what is known. A vision must not be allowed to become routinized or rusty.

2. *Transformed.* Transformation is the result of rule-governed and nonrandom processes. An acorn can be transformed into an oak tree and a cygnet into a swan, but no stone will become bread, no violence will bring peace, and no community without faith, hope, and love will ever produce a sustainable vision. It

will always be necessary, therefore, to strive to articulate the vision and to discern whether current structures and strategies have the capacity to keep it alive. A vision that is not transformed lacks the power to be life-giving. A transformed vision has power to inspire new generations.

3. *Comprehensible.* If a vision is unduly complicated, important details will be forgotten. A vision must be memorable. If people forget it, it simply cannot sustain them. The commitment of a treasure-seeker and a pearl-merchant offer a comprehensible vision of the kingdom.

4. *Imaginative.* We have already noted the critical importance of imagination. A vision must not be immediately within our grasp, yet not impossibly difficult to commit to. We need to be surprised and energized by the vision of what is already but not yet, a vision that can enrich lives.

5. *Relevant.* One of the saddest charges against Christianity and its ministers is that of irrelevance. The vision that sustains us and those we encounter must call us to encounter and engage with real people and real lives, so that they are changed for good. We must first do no harm to the lives of others, but surely we must try to ensure that the Good News we bear is not perceived as irrelevant.

6. *Embodied.* The vision cannot simply be proclaimed but must be lived. Jesus proclaimed the inbreaking of the realm of God through his whole life and work. Likewise, we can move ever closer to a realization of the vision by laying down our lives. It is very important indeed that those who lead communities and institutions are themselves willing and able to contribute to the realization of the vision by the integrity of their own lives.

7. *Collaborative.* Though the leader must lead and inspire, the vision is not simply the leader's conceptualization of what needs to be accomplished. Some leaders seem to deprive their communities of initiative and responsibility. But a collaborative vision is one that actually *requires* the work of others. There is

enough work for everyone; and no one should feel that he or she has no responsibility for sustaining the vision. A leader without followers is a voice in the wilderness.

8. *Passionate.* People will not be inspired by insipid ideas or unimaginative plans. There must be real passion, conviction, and commitment in our attempts to sustain the vision. As leadership passes from one person to another, so concerted efforts must be made lest the passion abate and the energy flag. Mutual trust must be built up; and where trust has been eroded it must be carefully restored and nurtured. Without trust there can be no passion. Without passion the vision dies.

9. *Risky.* A final, and crucial component of the vision is risk. Without a vision the people perish, and without something worth risking, the people have nothing worth living for, says Joan Chittister.[40]

LEADERSHIP FOR MINISTRY

How can we plan for the unknown and even for the unknowable? This paradox is one that we face as Christians attempting to live in faithfulness to Jesus yet not stuck in the past. If the Spirit of God is, as we profess to believe, attempting to renew the face of the earth, then we need to be attentive to the Spirit's promptings: otherwise we surely risk muzzling the Spirit. Little point exists in asking for signs and guidance if we are blind and deaf to the signs of the times. God is, indeed, trying to disturb us, to call our attention to God's will for the world.

As individual people and as members of communities of faith, we are not called to live in isolation but in solidarity. Leadership is necessary, whether concentrated or diffused, so that vision can be sustained, strategies can be discerned, and structures can be modified as needed. As we reflect on leadership styles, here are points for consideration and conversation.

In their landmark study, Nygren and Ukeritis[41] identified four types of leaders or leadership styles, which may be helpful to consider in the present context.

➤ *Value-based leadership* is found among those who see values but fail to create appropriate strategies. This leadership style would create a situation in which the vision is more like a dream or wishful thinking. Without strategies, the people are stranded.

➤ *Visionary leadership* exists where the leader—or a team, since the leader is not necessarily a single *factotum*—has both a strong vision and a set of appropriate strategies to implement that vision.

➤ *Conflicted leadership* would be characterized by an inability to handle changed and changing circumstances and would result in the leader's frustration, anger, or even despair, and the transmission of these emotions and sentiments to others.

➤ *Incognizant leadership* would be (blissfully, or crassly) unaware of significant issues and would thus fail to address them. Without aware leaders the people are like sheep without a shepherd.

The Nygren/Ukeritis study focuses on contemporary religious life in the United States, but its applicability in a number of areas is considerably wider. For example, it identifies two pairs of leadership styles and gives grades to each of these styles. Thus leadership may be characterized as *Transformational* or *Transactional,* and we may identify *Outstanding* or *Typical* leaders or leadership styles.

➤ *Transformational leadership* has the capacity to transform a community, always with the proviso that transformations are not miraculous but are limited by the raw material (though also graced by the Holy Spirit: but grace does build on nature). Such leadership does not stint with encouragement and praise. It articulates a vision. It links the vision explicitly to mission, both to God's mission and our own collaboration with God's mission. It instills a sense of corporate pride in the membership.

➤ *Transactional leadership* is less charismatic, less visionary, less mission-oriented. It establishes efficient and effective administrators and it maintains the institution. It identifies worthy projects and attainable goals. It rewards—and where necessary punishes—behavior. Some transactional leaders tend to avoid making decisions and even abdicate responsibility. One result, even of quite competent transactional leadership, is that the mission is mortgaged for maintenance, and the vision becomes obscured behind "projects."

➤ *Outstanding leadership* is committed to constant and solid improvement in all areas. It looks for new ways to achieve goals (perhaps imagination tanks would be of help here), involves membership as much as possible by attempting to build consensus, is not afraid to take initiatives and to influence the decisions and behavior of the group, and does not balk at problems and personnel that need to be addressed. A particularly notable characteristic of such leaders is their capacity and willingness to understand themselves as servants of God, the real leader of all good things.

➤ *Typical leaders,* by contrast, are more cautious and apt to fall back on their own resources, less likely to see themselves as servants and collaborators with the God who leads. Consequently, they are often too aware of their own limitations and adopt a negative or adversarial style of leadership. Adoption of this style may show itself in an overhasty invocation of sanctions or a precipitate use of formal authority. It may also manifest itself in denial of personal limitations and in an inability to consult and discern, thus producing regrettable and avoidable mistakes.

However, another kind of leadership lurks in the wings, sometimes called democratic or opinion-poll leadership. Here "the community's existing attitudes are the raw material of a leadership strategy; they are not the leader's script. Polls, though, are no substitute for leadership, because in its very essence leadership is about giving people what they *don't* already have—a sense of vision, inspiration, or even an adequate grasp of a particular subject. We need leaders to explain us to ourselves, to offer us ways of understanding our situation, and to propose creative solutions to our problems."

In Australia, the United States, Britain, and other countries today, there seems a dearth of moral leadership. Instead what has arisen is the opinion poll—what Australian political commentator Hugh Mackay called an "ugly development"[42]—not as a substitute for leadership but as an actual determinant of it. In religious life, such polls would inform leaders how to be popular by telling them what people want to hear and how they want to be led.

In the face of such trends, it is exceedingly important—for the Church on earth in whatever place and of whatever confession or community; for the survival of worshiping communities, and for the good of the Christian faithful—that there be strong and appropriate leadership. Otherwise, the vision of a faith-filled, committed, and vibrant people of God will fail to be sustained and the realm of God will not be proclaimed with appropriate passion and effectiveness.

SUMMARY

This chapter has considered some of the ways we may be creatively disturbed by God-inspired restlessness that turns our lives in new directions. We can move beyond a passive acquiescence in what is by asking *What if?* and *Why not?* as we seek an expanded range of moods for ministry. We can stimulate our imagination and encourage imaginative responses in others. We can work to keep a vision alive. We can strive to identify and encourage servant-leadership in our communities and churches. But all of these responses must be done creatively and constructively in an attempt to promote a more radical following of Jesus. Otherwise, our actions will ultimately fail to provide meaning to and relish for our lives, will lead to burnout, and will leave a bitter taste of disenchantment in our mouths.

We identified some factors that contribute to the maintenance of a life-giving and sustaining vision and considered the possibility that we are actually muzzling the Spirit in our times, with disastrous pastoral consequences. Later (in Chapter Six) we will consider the kinds of people who can contribute to a radical Christian witness by being a disturbing presence—one that is not irrelevant but truly life-giving, and one that simply cannot be ignored. First, however, we must acknowledge the scale of the challenge facing Christians today. A guard against cynicism and a corrective to self-destruction is the presence of an appropriate community. To this we turn next.

CHAPTER FOUR

Community, Communitas, and Downward Mobility

A CRITICAL CHOICE

S ome people seem to *impose* meaning on the world they encounter, while other people try to *expose* meaning, assuming that meaning is somehow there as part of the fabric of reality. Perhaps most of us combine the two approaches, believing that we can order the universe or external reality, but that we must also discover that meaning which is partially hidden. One thing is certain: in order to live in a meaningful way, everyone must make choices. As Viktor Frankl said, to live is to choose. The Jewish-Christian tradition has always valued this capacity to choose, and reminds us of the imperative: we must exercise this capacity rather than let it atrophy (Deut 30:15–20).

When a people no longer have the courage to undergo the pain required to choose the future over the past, then their institutions are compromised and their civilization is on its last legs. That statement is a paraphrase of one made by a Georgetown professor of world civilization, and it makes a very important point: every present generation must make a commitment to the future and to people, or risk contributing to the demise of the society of which it forms a part.

We have already noted the resilience of the Jewish people in the face (and aftermath) of the *Shoah*. Now, among the richer sections of industrialized societies we are watching those born since World War II as they struggle with their identity and try to determine what their own legacy to society will be.

The word "crisis" is from the Greek word *"krisis"* meaning a *sifting or separating*. The adjective form comes from the Greek word *"kritikos"* meaning *able to discern or decide*, from which the English word "critic" is derived. The Greek root of these group of words—*"krit"*—produces the word "criterion," a standard of judgment. Originally, therefore, this word carried overtones, not of foreboding or extreme danger, but of potentiality or creativity. We are told that the two characters, which together make up the written ideograph for crisis in the Chinese language, would be individually translated as *danger* and *opportunity*. Crisis certainly has elements of both.

South African missiologist David Bosch maintained that crisis is the normal situation for Christians throughout the ages. I believe he was implying that Christians are expected to make choices, to take responsibility, to discern and decide, and not simply to remain passive or reactive in the face of life's unfolding events. New Testament scholar Gerd Theissen,[43] writing of the early church, referred to "a general crisis of society..." and observed that not everyone is directly affected by societal crises but that certain groups are affected, *and these groups can exert an influence on the whole of society*. The time of Jesus saw various forms of religious revival of which one was the Jesus Movement itself which began as a branch of Judaism. As we shall see, it attracted people from marginal groups: "outsiders and eccentrics" in Theissen's phrase.

Is it not time, at the beginning of another age of waiting and working for the realm of God—or of unfulfilled expectation and cruel deception—for Christians to think and act differently? Is it not time to learn a lesson from the early church, to understand the potential within situations of crisis, and to take much greater responsibility for choosing the future over the past?

Those liberals whose agenda of the late twentieth century has proven to be virtually bankrupt promised a more responsible and grownup understanding of the faith and of Christian practice. They fell into the same trap, however, as all those who draw lines and rearrange the world. They proposed a Christianity that was rather too comfortable and middle-class, rather too tailored to individuals, rather too prone to forgetting or overlooking the radical challenge of Christianity, namely, the *challenge* of the Cross, without which the Cross loses its scandalous attraction (1 Cor 1:23–24).

There can be no authentic Christianity, no life-giving Christianity, no Christianity worth living and dying for without a daily taking up of the Cross and a following in the Golgotha-bound footsteps of the one who lived and died for us. This taking up of the Cross does not produce maudlin or miserable religion but offers abundant life to those with generosity of spirit, imagination, and daring (Jn 10:10). The Nygren/Ukeritis study[44] of contemporary religious life in the United States exposed some sad, but not altogether surprising, facts. One is this: that although religious communities virtually without exception identified themselves as dedicated to justice and to the needy, a very significant number of religious themselves failed to demonstrate this commitment in their daily lives.[45] This failure is not only a betrayal of what religious themselves profess, but grand larceny or theft of moral support and solidarity from the poor they are duty bound to serve. So what hope is there for the revitalization of Christianity and of Christians themselves? Can crisis produce new life? There is, of course, every hope, if we believe in the promises of Jesus. In that majestic Last Supper discourse, we recall his words:

Do not let your hearts be troubled.
Believe in God, believe also in me.

Very truly, I tell you, the one who believes in me
will also do the works as I do and, in fact,
will do greater works than these.

If in my name you ask me for anything, I will do it.

I will ask the Father,
and he will give you another
Advocate, to be with you forever.

Peace I leave with you; my peace I give to you.
I do not give to you as the world gives.
Do not let your hearts be troubled,
and do not let them be afraid.

If you abide in me,
and my words abide in you,
ask for whatever you wish,
and it will be done for you.

It is to your advantage that I go away,
for if I do not go away,
the Advocate will not come to you;
but if I go, I will send him to you.

Take courage; I have conquered the world.[46]

So much for the hope. What about the prospects for new life arising from current crisis? Christianity, not to mention Jesus Christ, was born in crisis, thrives in crisis, and should be deeply involved in crisis when Christ returns. Crisis is a time of discernment and decision; but discernment is a process that requires careful consideration, for it does not produce results by magic. Because decisions taken are not always wise decisions, crisis may lead to chaos as easily as to creativity. Crisis provides an opportunity for sifting: for sifting chaff from wheat, accidentals from essentials, and trappings from substance. Crisis affords us not just a moment but a context within which discernment and decisions are required. If there is a crisis of faith, then discernment and decisions must relate to faith itself. If the crisis is of confidence, authority, resources, or vision, then we cannot hope to come through the crisis with new life unless those specific issues have been addressed. We are not permitted to hunker down and hope for the crisis to pass: that is simply not worthy of Christians.

It would be utterly naive to imagine that all we have to do is keep on working, or looking busy, and hope the crisis will resolve itself. It was Hippocrates (460?-377? B.C.), who took the Greek word *"krisis"* and used it in a specifically medical context, to indicate the turning point of a disease. This usage was endorsed by Galen five hundred years later (A.D. 130?–200?): it thus came to connote *a grave condition, extreme illness.* In medical terminology, the crisis facing Christianity today may indeed be life-threatening. To keep on working as usual or to try and look busy may be the worst possible response. In medical terminology, a crisis requires critical or intensive care, and today's medical institutes provide highly specialized critical care. By analogy, critical situations in the church, in institutionalized religious life, or in the lives of the people of God cannot and must not remain unaddressed. Not only must they be confronted; they need particular or specialized treatment.

CRISIS AND COMMUNITY

When we think of the word "community," a number of images come to mind. We all have ideas, both of what community is or is not, and what it could be. If we can identify the distance between an actual community and the idea or ideal of community we have formed in our mind, we might be able to acknowledge some of the very real limitations of communities and even look for life-giving alternatives.

In a nontheological sense, dictionaries identify a number of components of community, as well as a number of different kinds of community. In the first place, the word "community" refers to people living in one locality or under one big roof. Community may actually apply either to the people or to the locality or to both. A community may also be a group of otherwise disparate people sharing a common cultural, religious, or ethnic identity. Beyond that, community refers to much broader concepts, such as the "European community" or the "Protestant community," which are really ideal types and much too big to be encountered as such.

Reflecting on the intentions of Jesus and his commission to

the Twelve, to the disciples in general, and by extension to the church, we notice that it is the community and not simply a single individual or a group of individuals that is commissioned. As sociologist Emile Durkheim (1858–1917) demonstrated, a community properly is not simply a group of people but a *corporate* group of people: a group that actually acts like a corporation or a single body. The Christian community is indeed and explicitly intended to be a corporate body, widely differentiated internally but with one head (Jesus Christ) and a unity of purpose.

This theology is elaborated splendidly by Saint Paul when he addresses abuses at Corinth and begs the fledgling community to live up to its high calling. The theology is further developed throughout the Pauline correspondence (For example, 1 Cor 12:12–30; Eph 4:3–13; Gal 3:26–28).

MECHANICAL AND ORGANIC SOLIDARITY

Durkheim explicitly—and implicitly Saint Paul before him—identified *mechanical* and *organic solidarity* as two very different forms of community. Mechanical solidarity might be what unites a school of fish or a colony of termites. Less attractively, it may describe the people at a parish liturgy. The fish and the termites might at least be said to have a common purpose, even though none of them individually actually has it in mind; the same cannot always be said for people who foregather for some liturgies.

By contrast, organic solidarity is expressed in the teamwork of a group of footballers or the marine exploits of the crew of an oceangoing yacht. Organic solidarity is manifested by a group of people acting in unison; and though each person has a different responsibility, the outcome of the whole group depends on the commitment of each individual.

Organic solidarity can produce world records and generate an indomitable spirit. Mechanical solidarity is not without possibilities, but those possibilities are predictable and less than inspiring. It is possible, though, for mechanical solidarity to lead to organic solidarity, providing there is trust, imagination, and something to galvanize the members of the group. Whatever the future of the institutional church may actually look like, it will only *have* a future if it develops its potential for organic solidarity, because mechanical solidarity simply does not have the capacity to meet the challenges of tomorrow.

Is it conceivable that the Christian churches as we have known them may have to undergo a very long winter, not in peaceful hibernation but in a fight for survival, before a new spring breaks through? The tension and the paradox is that the church worldwide, and in its many denominations, is an institution, and inevitably so, but that institutions are crippled by their own structures. Unless they slough the dead growth and regenerate, they die. Thus communities become institutionalized and suffer the same fate as any other institution. Unless they too undergo radical regeneration (in theological language, conversion or refounding), they slowly become sclerotic, and they too die. Many Christian churches are established as autonomous entities, whatever they proclaim about their desire for unity. How can the constituent communities of the Church remain in some communion, corporate and organic, in the face of forces of institutionalization and mechanical solidarity? Much more problematically, how can the unity for which Christ prayed ever become a reality?

Such unity can be achieved. In some measure it has already happened. But great clarity of purpose, vision, dedication, and living hope are required if there are to be further significant breakthroughs in Church unity. In the end there will have to be an ecclesial reality rather different from that which we are familiar, whether that be a universal united Christian Church or renewed and reinvigorated denominations and local congregations. Inevitably, Christians, too, will be rather different from those who are familiar to us, those who identify themselves as Christians yet fail to rise above intermittent expressions of mechanical solidarity. The Christian Church—and churches—of the future will, necessarily, be slimmed down and streamlined, if only because it is like leaven or light-source rather than great mass or raging wildfire. The Christian community will be once again as it was in the beginning, "a peculiar people."[47] If the Holy Spirit is allowed to come with fire and to renew the face of the earth, we simply cannot predict what the outcome will be because we are not God. But some strong clues exist in the New Testament—clues suggesting that forms of noninstitutional, ecumenical, and most certainly countercultural Christianity will abound. It will not be sufficient—indeed it never was—to call ourselves "Good Americans" or "Good Australians" or "Good Britons," and expect thereby automatic passage into the realm of God.

CREATION AND COMMUNITY

The popular image of the very first moment of creation—incandescent heat or the "big bang"—is an image of unharnessed, boundless, elemental energy. That image, transferred to a "founding moment" or, even earlier, to the actual Pentecost moment can raise our consciousness and ignite our imagination. In fact, ignition is another contemporary image that speaks of raw power and primal energy: "Ignition!" is the imperative mood that, at the touch of a button, can boost a rocket from inertia to supersonic speed in a matter of seconds.

Another simple thought-experiment will enable us to imagine that moment when the founder of a new religious movement—a religious order perhaps—transmits his or her dream to a handful of companions. The moment is brief, but its formative value, its effect on the small company and on an unsuspecting world, is immeasurable. The moment is characterized not only by its brevity but equally by its intensity and daring: the dream *must be* impossible, the companions *must be* insufficient, and the audacity of imagination or faith *must be* total. There is no room here for rational plans and equality of opportunity.

In 1703 in Paris, an idealistic twenty-three-year-old seminarian, with a handful of young students, imagined a world in which the penniless and exploited chimney sweeps of Paris would be cared for and protected. Between Claude-François Poullart des Places and this motley group there passed a kind of incandescent burst of energy, and from that moment their minds and hearts were fused round a common and impossible goal. What would become the Congregation of the Holy Ghost was born in that moment.

This occurrence is not unique: it is repeated, one might almost be tempted to say, routinely, at the founding moment of a hundred different congregations and orders, and of many other less canonical but no less creative undertakings. The common factors are outrageous imagination, insuperable odds, little practical likelihood of success (and thus high statistical probability of failure), and burning commitment both to the idea and to the community. This brief moment of incandescent energy generates what can be called "communitas." It is *not* a community in the usual sense. In fact, a small group of this kind, united in trust and committed to a Gospel ideal, fired by God's Spirit and launched on the adventure of a lifetime, is definitely not to be confused with a conventional community.

COMMUNITY AND COMMUNITAS

The power of communitas is fragile. It is not the power of the self-important. The power of communitas is to be found, paradoxically, in its vulnerability and modesty. The small group of people committed to undertaking a seemingly impossible task is touched not by hubris but by humility: the rootedness and groundedness of those who know their own very limited abilities, yet have abiding trust and enduring faith in the God of miracles. Communitas-power is not full of itself but is filled with nothing less than the power of God working through human instrumentality.

Communitas is the very opposite of structure: it is anti-structure. Its context is not organized routine or predictable timetable. When the impossible dream is captured by the group, no one would think of creating timetables as an organizational framework or job descriptions as a check on efficiency. On the contrary, meals will be infrequent and unscheduled, sleep a luxury, and comfort and security simply not an issue. "One for all and all for one" is the spirit that characterizes the group. Communitas is marked by zeal and energy, enthusiasm and collaboration. It actually generates a great deal of energy, because communitas is rooted in hope, united around a common vision, maintained by trust and inspired by great generosity. For a brief moment, a group experiencing communitas is both tireless and scheduleless. It is utopian, idealistic, and risk-taking.

Just as a flame struck from a flint surges, steadies, and slowly subsides, so does the incandescent power of communitas begin to abate even as its flame becomes visible. A match, once struck, will burn brightly only for an instant, for its relatively fierce heat and great light are already waning. It may be kept alive, even as it dies, if it is rotated and dipped so that the flame is sustained a little longer. And so it is with communitas: it lasts but a moment and then begins to die.

In those first days, when nothing is too much for the founding members and when energy is high, everyone is expended for the sake of the dream. But human beings cannot live like solar flares, and they seek a more sustainable life. At the moment when someone first suggests a modicum of rational organization—a fixed time for prayer, a regular schedule for meals, the distribution of responsibilities but, above all, a meeting—at that very moment communitas has become community. Community is the institutionalization of communitas and is as necessary as it is inevitable.

Communitas can carry people through moments of drama and high energy, risk and unpredictability; community sustains people for the long haul. Communitas produces the energy for takeoff; community sustains level flight. Communitas produces dreams and visions; community maintains works and programs that keep dreams alive and creates strategies that serve the vision. Communitas is ignited by a small group and is radical and pathbreaking; community is maintained by large numbers and is conservative and routine.

Both communitas and community are necessary for long-term undertakings. But in the long term, renewal can only come from a rediscovery of communitas, since community lacks the imagination and fire required by true conversion. Unless, however, the spark of communitas can be struck again and again from the flint of community, the momentum of a group will slow. The group will run out of ideas, its creativity will evaporate, and ultimately boredom and disinterest will replace inspiration and fire. Communitas is to community as the flame is to the coal, as the spark is to the flint, or as the fuel is to the rocket. Both are necessary, but the active agent is communitas. When the flame dies, when the spark fails, when the fuel is depleted, no coal will produce heat, no flint, flame, and no rocket, liftoff.

THE ENERGY AND INSPIRATION OF COMMUNITAS

There are religious communities today that pay for advertisements and pray for vocations. However, the only real success this strategy can produce is if, within the community itself, what is advertised is actually lived; if, in other words, the fire of communitas still burns. There are church officials today who speak of the equality of all and of collaboration among the people of God. But the only success this talk can produce is if, within the church itself, what is preached is actually practiced, if the fire of communitas still burns.

A community—or the church—may possibly attract rational human beings with rational plans and rational expectations, but only communitas can attract generous souls with hearts on fire and lives to lay down for a dream.

A community—or the church—in search of recruits may be looking to maintain itself and its works. If so, it needs rational people who can undertake rational tasks and sustain community projects.

On the other hand, a community—or the church—may be actively seeking to rekindle the fire that burned in the founding moment, generating heat and light that has now been lost. If so, it needs generous, creative, imaginative people whose zeal can be ignited by the vision of a daring and not quite rational undertaking. But communities—or the church—whose current membership is overtired, fragmented, and philosophically disunited are unlikely to attract generous, creative, and imaginative people.

If communitas-energy can be likened to incandescent fire and community-energy can be likened to the steadily burning but imperceptibly diminishing flame, it is not difficult to see what needs to be done in order to sustain the combustion. The second law of thermodynamics can help us here: it states, in essence, that heat or energy cannot be transferred from a cooler to a hotter body within a system. In other words, community-heat or community-energy lacks the capacity for combustion, because community itself represents a cooling down, a tendency toward equilibrium and indeed entropy—the loss of energy and the gradual breakdown of a system which leads to internal disorder. Consequently, only if communitas-energy can somehow be regenerated can the fire continue to burn and the light to shine.

When the flame of a burning match begins to flicker and show signs of dying we know the moment of incandescence that engulfed the match cannot be recaptured. Other matches may be struck, and other bursts of incandescence may be generated. Alternately, the dying match may be placed near kindling and the flame may perhaps catch again as it is taken up by dry wood. Still, in each case, the first incandescence will not be repeated and the uniqueness that was the light of that first match will be lost as the new fire takes hold.

But what if there is another match, not yet struck but ready for the striking? What if, instead of using energy to strike that second match against the rough surface, it is simply brought to the dying flame of the first match? Then there is reignition as the flame of the first match becomes the very flame of the second. New fire is created, but with all the energy of the old.

As a small boy I used to serve the early Mass at my parish in Manchester, England. In the wintertime, the coal fire in the kitchen at home would sometimes have survived the night, having been banked with dampened coal-dust or "slack" by my father as he went to bed.[48] Sometimes, in the morning, before leaving for Mass, I could fan it into flame, but not every day. Unless the ash *beneath* the fire had dropped through the grate—or was raked out so that the air could pass through the embers—the flame would not take hold. With no air to feed it, the fire inevitably died, even though it still retained some heat. I became quite proficient in riddling the grate and rekindling the fire. But there was a further lesson to learn: unless a critical mass of identifiable coal remained, and not simply a pile of hot ash, there would be nothing left after the riddling. With nothing to build on, there could be no reignition. Then I would return from Mass—to a cold and silent house—and have to set a new fire and start all over. I can still feel the cold and recall the shivers.

Could this experience offer an image for those disciples who want to find a way to carry forward, in a new form, a flame that was first ignited long ago? Such people do not simply want to warm their hands at the dying embers of an old fire or even to try to kindle a flame where there is only ash and memory. They want to see actual evidence of fire: then they will fan it so that it bursts into flames. Such people exist, of that there is no doubt. But many of them see in the contemporary church or contemporary religious life only the ash and the memory—or perhaps a dying ember. This residue is not worth living for, let alone worth dying for.

Communitas is characterized by high energy but not by numerical strength or physical power; on the contrary, communitas-energy is generated by, and in, a small, vulnerable, uncertain and socially insignificant group. Yet not every small, vulnerable, uncertain, and socially insignificant group will automatically produce communitas. A common dream, unity of purpose, deep commitment, idealism, daring, and indomitable hope—these are the indispensable ingredients of communitas. Something more is needed, however, without which the ingredients will never produce the kind of communitas that can change the world.

INITIATION AND COMMUNITAS

In traditional societies, when the time of initiation comes round, a group of young boys or adolescents (and this can apply with equal force to a group of girls) are removed from the routine of daily life to undergo a process of transformation. Ages of the peer-group members may vary by up to three or four years and occasionally more: but the group can truly be called an "age group." Children of chiefs and of rank-and-file community members together leave the security and predictability of the village for a period of separation and trial. They now become *liminal* or marginal: neither within nor completely outside the community (they are accompanied by senior adults, mentors, or midwives).[49] They will have an experience of life-changing importance, not only for themselves but also for, in particular, for the wider community, including the not-yet born. This experience is of communitas.

It is critically important for a community to assure continuity. It does so by socializing its members, turning the raw material (newborn infants) into the finished product (responsible adults). Initiation is one of the most important components of socialization, requiring people to pass through a formative stage of liminality, to forge an experience of communitas, and to reemerge as same-but-different and able to make a major contribution to the larger community.

In the experience of initiation, liminality and communitas converge. The former is expressed in the equality of everyone in the group: there is no hierarchy, no privilege, no single leader. On the contrary, there is a reduction, a leveling down, a stripping away of status. The boys or girls are without status or social identity, emptied of all they were and all they knew, so that they may be filled with all they will be and all they do not yet know. A kind of dying, a series of privations—of food, of sleep, of comfort, of predictability, and even of safety—is associated with this experience. At the end of it all, however, there will be a kind of rising, associated with indulgence—of food and clothing, of gifts and compliments, and particularly of status.

Those who went away as boys or girls returned transformed, as men and women: not biologically but socially, even spiritually. The status of child has been stripped from them, leaving them for a time without identity or place in the structure—liminal, marginal, "nobodies"—only to be replaced by the totally new status of adult. The bonding of these young people will have a profound impact on the broader society as these new adults take up responsibilities consistent with their status and become productive and reproductive providers and parents. This is by no means all that happens, for the liminality has also left each individual with an age-group of peers, formed by a common experience, fused by common memories, and committed to common ends. No longer are they marginal; now they are central to the community. No longer do they experience communitas; but as they become part of the mainstream community they remember the experience of transformation and commit themselves to the future and to life.

CREATIVE MARGINALITY AND DISCIPLESHIP

Jesus gathered a group of people around himself and withdrew with them periodically as he tried to turn them into something more: disciples. They were a group of peers, but still too interested in hierarchy and status. "What about us?" says Peter. "We have left everything and followed you." But Jesus offers them only intangible payment—with a bonus promise of persecutions (Mk 10.28–30). When they asked which among them was the greatest, Jesus pointedly declined to choose from among them: he called a child (marginal, liminal, a nobody who lacked status) over to them and told them to become like this child lest they be excluded from heaven (Mt 18:1–4). James and John persisted, asking to be seated to the right and left of Jesus; but in response he only promised a taste of his cup with its bitter dregs (Mk 10:35–40). And to drive home the point that hierarchy was not part of his plan, he stated unequivocally, "It is not so among you; but whoever wishes to become great among you must be your servant....For the Son of Man came not to be served but to serve, and to give his life a ransom for many" (Mk 10:43–45). This expression is one of intentional and creative marginality that can lead to life.

The little band gathered around Jesus has the quintessential experience of communitas. The group is small and its members are not very significant. Certainly they are not people of status or power. Its founder has a vision and an impossible dream, of a movement with minimal structure and no predictable routing. A scribe who wanted to join the group is told: "Foxes have holes, and birds of the air have nests; but the Son of Man has nowhere to lay his head" (Mt 8:20). Clearly, Jesus does not have an explicitly formulated rational plan, but he certainly does have a vision and a strategy.

Communitas attracts people who are "betwixt and between," marginal[50] to structure, and not the self-important or status-seeking. (Yet sometimes there are individuals in the group who have ambition and airs above their station: this will change as the liminal experience proceeds. The Twelve certainly show evidence of such ambition.) But though communitas requires people who may seem as though they have nothing to lose, it certainly does not offer them any easy options. Actually it demands their willingness to risk everything they have. They must be willing to gamble with their life. This potential for risk is precisely why communitas proves attractive to generous, noble souls: it is not that they have nothing to live for, but rather that they discover that they have everything to live for. No longer do they want to "save" their lives, as they might save money; now they want to "spend" their lives as they might celebrate an achievement. They do not want to lose their lives but to find them, and as Jesus promised, "Those who find their life will lose it, and those who lose their life for my sake will find it" (Mt 10:39).

Communitas requires liminal people, people committed to a common undertaking in a spirit of corporate solidarity and with no personal ambition. Lacking authority or status they are particularly able to carry universal moral values, to embody truth and justice and equality and compassion without any limitations. Because liminal people are neither inside nor outside but marginal, distinctions of insider/outsider or us/them do not exist: liminal people are best placed to become the inclusive "we." In fact, it is only by becoming a liminal person and by laying down or being deprived of personal status that one can actually begin to erase the barriers and boundaries that distinguish and divide people everywhere. Communitas is therefore intentionally countercultural, because culture needs distinctions and divisions, stratification and hierarchy, insiders and outsiders[51]—all of which are antithetical to communitas. Communitas is also utopian; or, better put, it is an illustration of the in-breaking of the realm of God. The story of the Good Samaritan exemplifies the dimension of liminality characteristic of communitas. The story starts with a person on the edge, crossing a boundary, neither insider nor outsider, as he travels between Jerusalem and Jericho. Having been attacked and robbed, he becomes even more liminal, hovering between life and death. The Good Samaritan was also a traveler, and certainly liminal to the people listening to Jesus tell the story. They were Jews (or gentiles) with very strong animosity toward Samaritans. Nevertheless, the Samaritan in this story not only acts nobly but puts to shame those socially significant people— the priest and the Levite—from whom more was to have been expected. It is not that the Samaritan has nothing to lose by helping a fellow traveler. Rather, he would have lost his own dignity and integrity had he failed to do so. It is not that he was unafraid of dying, but rather that he could not have lived with himself if he had failed to show compassion. And having made the point, Jesus said to the self-righteous lawyer, (and by extension, to those who hear the story): "Go and do likewise" (Lk 10:29–37).

Some people appear to want something that looks, at least superficially, like communitas. What actually may develop, however, is a community of servants or sycophants around one person who holds all the authority. This model is one of patron-and-client, and Jesus was quick to warn against it (Mt 20:25–28). The only way to avoid the crippling effects of dominant hierarchy is to counter them with dedicated service. Yet faith-filled pioneers, creative persons, generous souls, visionaries, and innovators also need communitas in order for the dream to continue and for the fire to burn brightly. However, communitas is like wine without a bottle: it needs some structure—community—so that it can be sustained over time. But community is like an uncorked bottle of wine: it needs communitas lest the flavor escape and the contents turn to vinegar. If communitas alone produces burnout, community alone will give rise to torpor.[52] Together they can animate and sustain the founding vision, but only if vigilance is exercised lest communitas become suffocated or community paralyzed.

PERMANENT LIMINALITY
AND DOWNWARD MOBILITY

Some wonderfully imaginative initiatives and clearly marginal ministries can, after a few generations, turn into comfortable and predictably routine operations. Once it was very dangerous to go to the "foreign missions." Between 1859 and 1900 the life expectancy of young missionaries (Holy Ghost Fathers, Spiritans) embarking for Sierra Leone, West Africa, was less than ten months, and the average missionary died before reaching thirty years of age. But there were always more people waiting to replace the missionaries who died.

In the nineteenth century, women like Cornelia Connolly of the Sisters of the Holy Child Jesus, Anne-Marie Javouhey of the Sisters of St. Joseph of Cluny, or Katharine Drexel of the Sisters of the Blessed Sacrament pioneered girls' education and inspired generations of women to rise to the challenge in less than hospitable environments in North America, Europe, Africa, and on Native American Reservations.

Today the life expectancy of those in overseas ministry is comparable to that of those at home, while girls' education no longer needs pioneers. Still, today's ministry, wherever it may be, cries out for dedicated teachers willing to commit to marginal situations; and, meanwhile, a host of new pioneer situations have arisen—from AIDS care to hospice, from rehabilitation of child soldiers to ministry among child prostitutes. The successors of the Spiritans—or of the Connollys, Javouheys, and Drexels—are not as numerous now; but those who remain must rekindle the fire if they are to be credible and creditable sons and daughters of their founders; and other inspired people—women and men—must step forward as advocates for today's needy and forgotten people. This replenishment of the ranks is so, simply because such dedication and initiative is the lifeblood of Christianity. Without it, Christianity would deserve to die.

The fastest-growing group of people on earth today is the poor. Even in the United States, there are more than thirty million people below the poverty line; they are dying, not immediately but by degrees. Worldwide, more than a billion people are in abject poverty, dying with every breath they take. A curious statistic appeared recently. Less than twenty years ago, the very rich were estimated to have fifty times as much as the very poor; now they possess seventy-two times as much. Those figures represent such a gap as to be almost meaningless, but they illustrate a highly significant point. With every single increment in our standard of living, every single decimal point of upward mobility, we are thereby falling further away from the poor, to whom we, as Christians, have a responsibility in justice. It is not enough for us to claim that we cannot do anything: we can, and must, do something. Simply because we cannot do everything does not give us permission to do nothing; and if we do nothing positive, we are doing something negative: we are sinning by omission.

In the twentieth century, life expectancy for people in the privileged nations increased by almost 70 percent—an unprecedented and unrepeatable factor. In 1900, women's life expectancy in the U.S. and Europe was around forty-seven years, and men's a little less, at forty-six. In the year 2000, the life expectancy of women in the U.S. and across Europe had risen to around eighty years, while men's was further back, at around seventy-six.[53] In 2000, the life expectancy for all people in Ethiopia was actually less than forty years (Pears Factfinder 2002, Penguin Books, New York, 2001); and with war, AIDS, and genocide accounting for so many deaths in Africa, life expectancy in several countries on that continent was less than in Europe a century ago.

History will hold the rich nations accountable for the decimation of nations through AIDS and genocide. Their apathy, dressed as nonintervention, is an abdication of moral responsibility. And as a small percentage of the world's population can choose retirement-with-benefits around the age of fifty and expect the benefits to last them another thirty years or more, a huge percentage of the world's population has neither the hope of retirement-with-benefits nor even the expectation of life beyond the immediate future.

If we bring the earlier reflections—about communitas and

creativity, liminality and loving service—into engagement with these brief reflections on contemporary needs and the faces of injustice, we should be able to draw some conclusions that can be applied to our own lives as disciples.

DISCIPLESHIP TRANSFORMED

Jesus tried to transform his own disciples by leading them to faith and by exemplifying kenotic ministry, egalitarianism, and service. The word "kenosis" refers to the self-emptying of Jesus as shown in the Letter to the Philippians (Phil 2:6–7). Kenotic ministry is the opposite of pompous self-importance. We are called to follow Jesus in this way. In our day, transformation is often identified more in terms of self-actualization or personal goals than in terms of self-transcendence and service. The face of Christianity in the very near future will have to reflect the life of Jesus much more than it currently does, and exhibit much less of the face of respectable and self-focused individuals than it currently does. Not everyone will be able to sustain the dream of Jesus. But those who do will need to find new forms of communitas, leading to new ways of service. Indeed, without new forms of communitas there cannot be new ways of service.

In the past, people went overseas without expecting to return: theirs was a ministry of permanent liminality expressed in permanent separation from their homeland. In the future, permanent liminality will be no less important but will be expressed rather differently. There will continue to be a need to leave home, but there is an increasing need actually within the homeland, right under our noses, where people are forcibly marginalized, or where they experience passive marginalization whether because of ethnicity, religion, sexual orientation, medical history, age, or any number of other frontiers of exclusion.

In the future—which effectively means today's commitment carried into tomorrow—the need for permanent liminality and downward mobility becomes as keen and as clear as it was when Jesus first struck that spark and released a burst of incandescent energy. His own life was one of permanent liminality and downward mobility, for there could be no half measures and no temporary commitment to justice and compassion.

At this juncture in history, there is great need for people to choose liminality or active marginalization. For those with sufficient strength of character there is much to do. If the Holy Spirit is allowed to lead the church, perhaps some currently developing forms of discipleship will lead us far beyond canonical vows and institutionalized community to other forms of intentional commitment expressed as communitas. Perhaps disciples will continue to leave their safe havens and move to the boundaries in service of those whose lives are eked out there. Perhaps new prophets and witnesses to the realm of God and the hope expressed by and in Jesus will arise far from the centers of theological respectability and conventional vocations.

There is already imagination and trust to be found in individuals and small groups hungry and thirsty for justice. The official church may fail to recognize them or may attempt to control them, but if they are of God they will prevail. Institutionally, the Roman Catholic church—and this appears to be widely true of other denominations—is suffering from simultaneous crises (dangers and opportunities): there is a crisis of credibility, a crisis of authority, a crisis of creativity, and a crisis of imagination, to name but four. Unless the various churches are alert to the presence of generous and imaginative souls, they will be guilty of failing to seize the day and guilty of failing to read the signs of the times.

Without the encouragement of imagination by those with ecclesial responsibility and authority, there will only be workers where there should be witnesses, and only the dwindling professed where there should be the doughty prophets. Without imagination, the future will only be a pale repetition of the past, a sure death warrant not only for religious life but for all creative ministry in the church. Demoralized people either do nothing until they die, or they change allegiance before it is too late. It is not true that where there's life there's hope, but it is true that where there's hope there's life.

Somehow, Jesus managed to keep hope alive, and to transmit a glimpse of his great idea to his disciples and to the later followers of The Way. Somehow that idea (as Gerard Manley Hopkins described the Spirit's action) "flamed out like shook foil" in that first Pentecost. Somehow it has continued to burn, in spite of the ash and the lack of air that threaten to extinguish it. Somehow the early disciples discovered the power and compelling attraction of the vision of Jesus and its incandescent power. Somehow they kept it alive. Somehow we have to do the same.

Summary

In these pages we have looked at crisis, at solidarity, and a different kinds of community. Communitas is the experience of something so worth living for as to be worth dying for. Communitas is the encounter with others that can give life a deeper meaning. We need to seek communitas possibilities in order to retain our deep *joie de vivre*. With communitas as the fire at the core of our lives, we can be inspired to undertake downward mobility as a way to warm other people's hearts, if not strike the flame in their lives as well. To see how this can be a possibility for ourselves, we will look at how it was a reality in the life of Jesus.

CHAPTER FIVE

The Disturbing Ministry of Jesus

INTRODUCTION

The ministry of Jesus confirms what Viktor Frankl maintained: that to love you must encounter. Jesus' ministry could be described as loving encounter. He moved beyond familiar reference points, broke through boundaries, and reached out without discrimination to all the people. At the same time Jesus disturbed the status quo and challenged the complacent. His ministry was not what many people expected, and he did not flatter civil and religious society. He repudiated the notion that some people are more worthy than others, and he deliberately called to those judged less worthy of God's love. The essential message of Jesus, however, is one of unification and reconciliation, of outreach and inclusion. No one, in principle, is excluded.

To those with a romantic idea of "gentle Jesus, meek and mild," the image of Jesus in the New Testament will come as something of a shock. Jesus is undoubtedly a disturbing figure; but if we have the imagination of Wordsworth and the faith of our ancestors, we will relish the challenge made to his disciples. Then, having been captivated by his boundary-breaking, healing ministry, we may have the courage to put our hand to the plow and to move forward in his footsteps, to encounter through love, to oppose discrimination, to do justice, and to proclaim the realm of God. If, in so doing, we also become a disturbing presence, we have reason to believe it will also be creative and life-giving.

NATURE AND CULTURE

In the first creation story of the Book of Genesis we are offered a glimpse of the way things should be: man and woman, male and female are created in God's own image, *and equally so* (Gen 1:27). In the second creation story, we are reminded of the complementarity of the couple: the two are one body, one flesh (Gen 2:24). And in the Christian dispensation, the writer of Matthew's Gospel applies this ancient tradition explicitly to marriage: "what God has joined together, let no one separate" (Mt 19:6).

The creation stories attest to the integrity of the whole of creation. God established a harmonious world and warned humanity to respect the Creator's intentions. If we look carefully, we will notice that from the very beginning patterns and values—of mutuality, interrelatedness and respect—are clearly visible. This example from Genesis presents a very clear and strong *worldview*: a glimpse of the way things should be.

Yet almost from the beginning, darker forces and countercurrents were also at work: disobedience and arrogance were incipient hallmarks of humanity. As the Book of Genesis tells it, the man and the woman disturbed the harmony of paradise, alienated themselves from the Creator, and established an ambiguous relationship between themselves and the rest of creation. God says to Adam: "By the sweat of your face / you shall eat bread / until you return to the ground, / for out of it you were taken; you are dust, / and to dust you shall return" (Gen 3:19). At this moment of divine displeasure, the man and the woman were certainly aware of the disturbing presence of God.

In that very stirring narrative, the epic story of humanity is distilled. First, the primordial chaos is reorganized by the Creator, who establishes an enclave of order and integrity. Then, for a brief moment there is concord between Creator, humanity, and the rest of creation. But a sudden catastrophe turns harmony into havoc, and a perfect world is undermined by discord and distress. In the less lofty language of postmodernity, we might say that paradise represents an impossible, mythical state of bliss. It is maintained by omnipotent divinity and characterized by the promise of integration and peace. In fact, the strong *world-view* of the Genesis story is clearly utopian: it cannot be realized outside paradise. By contrast, the *ethos* we actually experience—the real world in which we actually live—is far from utopian and rather closer to chaos. It is maintained by arrogant humanity and characterized by the threat of disintegration and discord. In other words, *paradise* is to *the real world* as *nature* is to *culture*. And that, in a profound sense, is where the trouble starts.

Culture is what humanity does to the world in which it lives. Culture requires the very sundering of nature, the very separation and division that the Book of Genesis expressly warns against. The survival of culture demands the naming and taming of nature. Culture is always, to some degree, at odds with nature; culture is always at some odds with the Creator. These statements are not hyperbole; they are a measure of the hubris of humanity. In theological language, this hubris may be the original sin.

Historical humanity, of course, does not and cannot exist in a pure state of nature. Culture is *cultivation,* modifying the environment by controlling nature. The irony, or paradox, is that despite immense technological creativity, humanity seems incapable of discovering or creating really balanced or harmonious worlds, much less an actual Garden of Eden. Cultures are built on a latticework of separation and division, classification and categorization, discrimination and domination. Rational and accomplished though human societies may be, they are, universally, built upon untruths or the manipulation of reality: in short, lies.

Yet even "in the beginning"—in that mythic moment we call *illo tempore*, which is not historical time but timeless time or sacred time—there are indications of "culture" in the midst of nature. Having created everything out of the common ground from which humanity also sprang, God brought all the living things before Adam so that he could give them names (Gen 2:19–20).

To name something or someone is to exercise power over it. By itself, power is simply a capacity to accomplish something. But power that is legitimated becomes authority, and in the Genesis story God is giving Adam real authority. The act of naming actually classifies and separates things, so Adam is responsible for classifying the created world. This is an awesome power, and at this point in the story, it is good.

After the Fall, however, things change drastically. As a result of disobedience, the harmony of nature is disturbed, the mutuality between the man and the woman is undermined, and even the relationship between humanity and God is compromised. Before very long, the tragic break between humanity and God, and between humanity and creation, has produced the tragic fragmentation of humanity itself, when Cain murders his own brother Abel (Gen 4:8). What God has united, humanity has now effectively divided.

THE CULTURAL FLAW:
CONSEQUENCES OF THE ORIGINAL SIN

The first time someone separates people by drawing a real or symbolic line between them, and the first time someone makes a moral judgment in choosing between people, at that moment the world has become divided where previously it was not. This act of division leads to dominance and destruction, inclusion and exclusion, hierarchy and privilege. It also leads to the development of culture.

The survival of humanity, or human beings in groups, is predicated upon the ability to name and tame the world. But the very first line of discrimination and division is at the same time a sword that strikes at the unity and integrity of humanity. As soon as people can distinguish "us" and "them," they have undermined and split the unitary category "we."

However, one does need to be careful here. History illustrates the sad truth that if people are too naive, and if they assume they are all one happy family, there is a serious danger that those they considered part of "we" may in fact prove hostile, thereby establishing themselves as "them"—and even threatening to exterminate "us." This constant tension between the desire for inclusion and the intuition for exclusion characterizes humanity. However strong our better instincts may be, the imperative of self-preservation seems to compel people to draw lines. But unless people are truly inclusive on a universal scale, the very lines that include will also serve to exclude. Without mutual trust, people's differences will come to outweigh their similarities.

Even if the line between "us" and "them" is initially drawn for purely practical purposes ("we can't invite *everyone* to the wedding"), there is a social tendency for more than notional distinctions ("some of my best friends are Jewish/Protestant/rich") to develop. Then, increasingly, objectified boundaries ("strong fences make good neighbors") may be erected. Before long, "us" and "them" are separated by real, if invisible, barriers. Warren Zimmerman, former U. S. Ambassador to Yugoslavia, spoke of "borders of the mind"—those invisible but very real barriers that separate people: barriers of superiority, hatred, bigotry, and so on.

Sometimes, people on either side of invisible borders manage to live in peaceful coexistence, though not in true harmony. At other times, differences harden into disagreements, or people come to blows, or worse. Again, where adjacent communities have difficulty in living side by side, but each is equally committed to survival, they may actually arrange for some kind of mutual exchange, the most effective form of which is intermarriage. In this way, groups of people who are hostile in one generation may become amicable in a subsequent generation if their children intermarry and produce children whose grandparents were at odds. Marriage and similar forms of bonding or covenant may, in the course of time, succeed in turning enemies into friends.

Cultural and Social Polarities: Us and Them

There is a human tendency to create groups that become both self-defined (inclusive) and polarized against other groups (exclusive), as well as inward-looking (centripetal) and outward-looking (centrifugal). This tendency, curiously enough, applies not simply at the macro-level but at the micro-level as well. At the macro-level it is fairly obvious. For example, to establish the identity of the English and the Irish, to distinguish Americans from Canadians, or to discriminate between people of different religious denominations, political parties, or ethnicities is to draw lines of inclusion and exclusion, markers of "us" and "them." But the same principle also applies at the micro-level: among the English themselves (and equally among the Irish, Americans, and Canadians), other lines may be drawn: lines that divide and discriminate internally. Let's look at this.

Take the English, among whom I count myself: they are as good as any in drawing both vertical and horizontal lines. Sometimes they identify themselves with other English people, while comparing and contrasting themselves with the Scots or Welsh or Irish. (We could indicate this graphically by drawing a vertical line of separation, whether literally or figuratively: medieval castles, "the Pale" in Ireland, or even the *English* Channel, are examples). But English people are also capable of drawing attention to the differences between themselves—whether of social class, gender, age, wealth, or whatever. (We could indicate this by a horizontal line of separation: it could serve to segregate people by access to London Clubs, expensive hotels, or formal nights at Covent Garden Opera House.)

Much of what the English are capable of in this respect is true of virtually every other definable group of human beings. This amounts to a cultural propensity for inclusion and exclusion, hospitality and xenophobia, equity and discrimination, and so on.[54] We might indicate this by creating a cultural grid (fig. 1).

In this grid, the thick vertical line separates insiders ("us") from outsiders ("them"), while the horizontal line distinguishes two categories: participants and nonparticipants. Thus the cultural grid produces four numbered quadrants, each of which has an internal identity but is also separated—more or less—from the other three quadrants. This cultural grid can, in principle, be applied to any and every human culture, whether past or present.

FIG. 1

	US	**THEM**
PARTICIPANT	PARTICIPANT INSIDERS 1	4 PARTICIPANT OUTSIDERS
NONPARTICIPANT	2 NONPARTICIPANT INSIDERS	3 NONPARTICIPANT OUTSIDERS

What distinguishes cultures is both the nature of the horizontal and vertical lines in each case and their placement relative to particular configurations of population. The vertical line could move to the left, thus restricting the group of insiders and expanding the group of outsiders; or it could move further to the right, with the opposite effect. Likewise, the horizontal line could move up, thus defining a smaller group of participants (whether insiders or outsiders); or down, thus expanding the participants relative to the nonparticipants (see fig. 4. on pp. 102–103).

No less significant than the positioning of the vertical and horizontal lines is their effect on the categories or quadrants they thereby create. The Great Wall of China, the Iron Curtain, or the Berlin Wall—or natural barriers like the Amazon or the English Channel—are very effective means of separating "us" and "them." The Thirty-Eighth Parallel, the Mason-Dixon line, or the border between Mexico and the United States represent highly effective and well-patrolled lines of separation. As well, the isolation of an island, large or small, constitutes a very effective boundary. The fact that walls, rivers, or national borders also serve to enclose, protect, and identify groups of people should also be noted. Strong borders or boundaries serve to create strong social identities.

In contrast, we might think of neighbors whose property is *not* marked by high walls or natural barriers or of people and communities who live without fear and who have always felt free to wander, explore, and encounter others. The so-called European Community is a recent experiment—or invention—aimed at dismantling historical frontiers and dissolving long-standing animosities. Its effectiveness depends not on politicians alone but on people generally. Likewise, some churches, separated historically by powerful symbolic barriers, have more recently shifted the emphasis from what differentiates them to what unites them with the result that the barriers have begun to crumble. By contrast, the Roman Catholic church appears to be refining some tests of orthodoxy and attempting to build ever-higher walls to mark its theological and disciplinary territory. If this observation is correct, it is a good way for the church to demarcate its identity from an internal perspective as well as an effective way to isolate itself from the wider world. This demarcation is a typical characteristic of a sect.

So far we have discussed the vertical lines that reinforce or undermine the differences between "us" and "them." The horizontal lines may likewise be more or less patrolled, more or less exclusionary in effect.

In a highly stratified society where privilege is for the few and where the masses outnumber the elite, the horizontal line of separation between participants and nonparticipants will be defended with great vigor. The Roman Empire maintained borders and fortresses (the vertical line of defense against the barbarians or other outsiders) but also amassed legal entitlements and privileges (the horizontal lines in defense of favor and honor against the common people, noncitizens, slaves—and women).

By contrast, in more egalitarian societies, the horizontal line may be more tentative and less strongly drawn. In that case, some nonparticipants may even be able to raise their heads above the crowd and aspire to a measure of upward mobility, which may allow them some access into the world of the participant insiders. The American Dream was of a society without horizontal lines: unstratified, lacking in special privilege or class distinction. However, a measure of the pervasiveness of the human tendency to draw lines and to discriminate is the fact that even in the United States there are, in practice, palpable distinctions between different groups and categories of people who aspire to be "one nation under God."

JESUS AND THE CULTURAL GRID

At this point, we can identify each of the four quadrants of the cultural grid and use this tool explicitly to consider the implications of the message of Jesus for his own society, and also to consider the challenge of Christianity to every nation under heaven and every culture on earth.

First, a preliminary and highly significant point must be made. In every case, it is the insider participants[55] (occupants of quadrant #1) who effectively determine three things: where the line between insiders and outsiders is drawn, where the line between insider participants and insider nonparticipants is drawn, and how porous or nonporous the lines will be. By way of example, we might imagine a number of religious worlds, religious enclaves, or ecclesiastical communities.

FIG. 2

INSIDER PARTICIPANTS	OUTSIDERS
INSIDER NONPARTICIPANTS	

We may begin by visualizing a religious world (fig. 2) in which the occupants of the top left-hand quadrant (the insider participants) might be the clergy in general or the hierarchy in particular (by virtue of social status). They would establish an exclusionary zone whose borders would be patrolled by upholders of strict orthodoxy and executors of appropriate sanctions, as well as by no more than a handful of people who would declare what the will of God is, and who would even utter absolute statements about the very mind of God. In such a world, the insider participants would be a very small elite, while the insider nonparticipants would not only be the vast majority of the community, but would almost all be excluded from aspiring to the ranks of the insider participants. A very small number of people would be carefully prepared for upward mobility into the ranks of the insider participants, but only after very careful vetting and assurances of faithful conformity and loyalty. However, not all insider participants are self-serving: the kenotic ministry of Jesus illustrates the possibility of moving from the centers of privilege to the margins or boundaries where missionary encounters take place.

As to the line between insiders and outsiders, it could be more or less porous. Insiders would expect to enjoy freedom to come and go at will, and outsiders might be invited to approach; but outsiders would only be able to become insiders with some difficulty, and after major modifications to their lifestyle. Even if some outsiders should aspire to assimilation, they would hardly ever become insider participants but only insider non-participants.

The religious world we are visualizing here is not a purely hypothetical world, nor is it an actual world. But is a possible world. A radically alternative religious world could also be imagined. In this one (fig. 2), there would be a line between insiders and outsiders, but it would be more notional than real, more porous than watertight. Similarly, the line between insider participants and insider nonparticipants would not be patrolled, except to attempt to erase it and invite increasing participation from as many people as possible. The quadrants would then look more like this (fig. 3):

FIG. 3

INSIDER PARTICIPANTS	OUTSIDER PARTICIPANTS
INSIDER NONPARTICIPANTS	OUTSIDER NONPARTICIPANTS

At this point, it should be fairly easy to apply this flexible grid to any number of actual societies and to demonstrate a huge variety, both in terms of where the vertical and horizontal axes intersect, and in terms of the strength or weakness of the boundary lines. Thus we could envision figure 4.

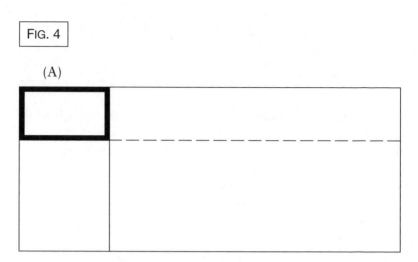

(A)

Society (A) is comprised of an exclusive group of insider participants, strongly defending all boundaries. This is an enclave or an oligarchy, but certainly not an open democracy. The participant insiders may feel safe, but they are also effectively isolated.

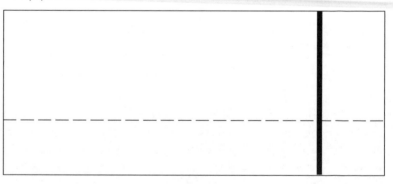

(B)

Society (B) is strongly resistant to strangers, no matter what their qualifications, but is internally open and allows people to move from status to status. The number of dependent people or "nobodies" is comparatively small.

(C)

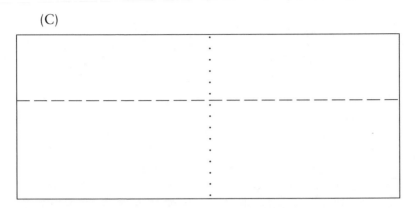

Society (C) appears equally open to all. Unlike society (B) it does not raise barriers against outsiders (it is not xenophobic). Yet it is potentially vulnerable both from within and from without.

(D)

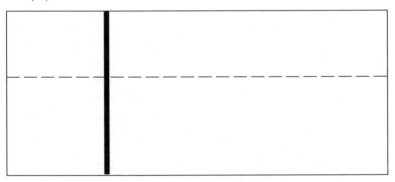

Society (D) is privileged and has taken pains to defend itself against outsiders. It has signs of a siege mentality relative to the outside world but is internally egalitarian.

THE DISTURBING PRESENCE OF JESUS

Having now developed a model, we can apply it to the ministry of Jesus; and at the same time, we can learn something about the challenge that faces everyone who attempts to be a disciple of Jesus, one who goes in the name of the Lord.

The social and religious environment (that is, the culture) in which Jesus exercised his ministry looked very much like (A) in fig. 4 on page 102. A tight, powerful, and defensive group of religious leaders—typified in the High Priest, the scribes, and the Pharisees—supported a strong religious world, maintained by religious rules and sanctions. Many of the local people—Jews at least nominally (insiders)—were considered good for nothing: "nobodies" (in John Dominic Crossan's word), "the last" (in the words of Jesus), and certainly insignificant, nonentities, and largely incapable of ever achieving religious respectability. The barrier between the insider participants and the insider nonparticipants was such that salvation was believed to be restricted to an exceedingly small and privileged group of keepers of the law and the Sabbath.

A few examples will serve. An adulterous woman was seen not only as a sinner but as forever excluded from God's mercy. In principle she could repent, make retribution, and begin again, but the only way she *could have* made retribution (by paying a large fine) was barred to her, since her ill-gotten gains were contaminated and totally unsuitable for this purpose. A leper was permanently impure and could never be religiously acceptable—unless, of course, the leprosy were reversed and the leper were to receive a certificate of purity from one of the priests: a virtual impossibility. A criminal, such as a thief, had little hope of ever regaining respectability in a world dominated by codes of honor and shame. In addition, infants and children—especially girl children—were simply insignificant because they were immature and unproductive. Some (usually boys) would grow up to become insider participants, but many (usually girls) would not, and others (deviants, the powerless) would permanently constitute "the poor" who were always around.

Such, in brief, was the religious climate at the time of Jesus. However, there was another world, too, with other rules and sanctions. This world was one in which politics, ethnic identities, and national aspirations were played out. Here could be felt the authority of an occupying power and the reaction of a beleaguered people. In such a context, the difference between insiders and outsiders was clear, yet the line between them was not entirely within the control of the insiders.

When people are subject to an occupying power—as were the French between 1940 and 1945, or the Native American people in the days of the westward migrations—there may be a resistance movement as well as instances of collaboration. Certainly there will be unrest, confusion, and attempts to find some security in a threatening world. Diagram D in figure 4 (p. 103) is one expression of this kind of reaction against outsiders.

How, then, can we characterize the cultural context and pastoral strategy of Jesus? Figure 5 (p. 106) represents only the two left-hand sections (insiders) of the four-quadrant model represented in the previous figures (quadrants 1 and 2). A number of observations can be made.

Fig. 5	INSIDERS

P
A
R
T
I
C
I
P
A
N
T
S
	Adult Males/VIPs:
	
	Holders of authority (legitimated authorization) and power (strength, control, dominance)
	
	• ***Significant others; legitimators:***
	   • HEADS OF HOUSEHOLDS
	   • MEMBERS OF PROFESSIONS
	    Physicians, Financiers/Bankers, Lawyers, Clergy, Teachers.
	   • APPOINTED/ELECTED LEADERS
	
	• ***Those with power of sanction***
	   • MILITARY, CIVIL DEFENSE, POLICE
	   • RELIGIOUS AUTHORITIES
	   • POLITICAL/LEGAL AUTHORITIES

N O N
 	
P
A
R
T
I
C
I
P
A
N
T
S
	Non-Adult Males/Nobodies:
	
	People without authority (no social identity) and with limited power (though not completely powerless)
	
	• ***The immature***
	   • *The unborn: lacking viability*
	   • *Infants: lacking language*
	   • *Children: lacking sexual maturity*
	
	• ***The deviant***
	   • *Physically: cripples, the sick*
	   • *Mentally: the insane, crazy, possessed*
	   • *Morally: criminals, prostitutes, tax collectors, "sinners"*
	
	• ***Women***
	
	• ***Nonparticipating males***

There are insider participants and insider nonparticipants separated in this diagram by a horizontal line, but in reality by barriers that are more or less objective and more or less negotiable. That is to say, every actual social system operates with an invisible but real horizontal line of demarcation, but the nature of that line or boundary varies widely. Some societies operate in a more relaxed manner, while others are strongly committed to maintaining the distinction between insider participants and insider nonparticipants. This distinction is something we not only encounter in the world of the New Testament but in every social world, including our own.

Consider the world in which Jesus was to exercise his adult ministry. Some have imagined him among the insider participants: after all, he was an adult male, he was called rabbi or teacher, and he claimed to be of David's line. We might, therefore, argue for Jesus' insider-participant status. However, he was also a peasant carpenter from Nazareth in Galilee, of which Nathanael asked rather scornfully: "Can anything good come out of Nazareth?" (Jn 1:46). Furthermore, he appeared not as a husband or father but as an itinerant who went around with a motley group of other "nobodies." He was no respecter of persons and was sometimes deeply critical of the "establishment." We could certainly argue, therefore, for the nonparticipant status of Jesus.

JESUS AS OUTSIDER

We could do more. We could argue that Jesus was actually an outsider, and by choice.[56] He seemed to be attracted by the margins of society and the marginalized people to be found there. He was forever wandering on the borders and crossing boundaries. He crossed geographical boundaries as he journeyed between Galilee and Samaria, the Decapolis, Judea, or Transjordania (Mt 4:25), religious boundaries as he moved from synagogues to graveyards, and topographical boundaries as he sailed on lakes, climbed mountains, or was led into a desert.

Moreover, not all the boundary experiences of Jesus were entirely under his control or undertaken at his initiative. One thinks of the encounter with the Samaritan woman at the well (Jn 4:5ff) or the Syrophoenician women who pleaded on behalf of her daughter and herself (Mt 15:21). Jesus' ministry transcended other boundaries, too, such as the invisible boundaries that protected zones of privilege, exclusiveness, or holiness.

If we visualize Jesus as originally located close to the intersection which separated insiders and outsiders, participants and nonparticipants (for he was never to be found ensconced at the center of privilege or power), we can see him gathering his little band of followers and stepping over the line separating insiders and outsiders and choosing the social identity of outsider. For any minister in the spirit of Jesus, this choice itself is worth pondering: Jesus was "a marginal Jew"[57] in a double sense: both a person who lived on the margins and a Jew who was somewhat marginal to the religious establishment of his day. To contemporary Christians this reflection is critical, and among the many biblical references in support of it, two in particular are worth mentioning.

First, in one of his letters, Saint Paul refers to Jesus, whose insider-participant status in the divine household was unquestionable: in fact he "was in the form of God… / as something to be exploited, / but emptied himself, / taking the form of a slave, / being born in human likeness. / And being found in human form, / he humbled himself / and became obedient to the point of death— / even death on a cross (Phil 2:6–8). A slave is clearly a nonparticipant; a person who dies by crucifixion is a nonparticipant par excellence.

Second, in the passage on the Last Judgment, to which we will return in the next chapter, the evangelist identifies Jesus as saying quite clearly, "I was a stranger" (Mt 25:35). It is ironic—if understandable—that Christians have always struggled to accept the self-emptying or kenotic ministry that so characterized Jesus, just as it is understandable that Christians should have chosen to make a virtue of being kind to strangers, though few would follow the example of Jesus and actually choose to become strangers themselves.

Revelation—God's outpouring of self-disclosure—tends to unite, and includes of all humanity. Religion—what humanity makes of God's revelation—tends to divide and becomes exclusive. "Religion (in the eyes of the stringently pious) said that the table-fellowship of Jesus with the ritually or morally unclean, communicated uncleanness to Jesus himself. Jesus, of course [God's revelation], saw it the other way round: he was communicating salvation to religious outcasts."[58]

THE CHALLENGE OF JESUS

From the freely chosen position of outsider, Jesus can mix with, and perhaps even gather round himself other outsiders, whether Samaritan (Lk 9:51–56; Jn 4), Syrophoenician (Mt 15:21–28), or fellow Galileans like Peter and Andrew or James and John (Mt 4:18–22). Some refused, of course, like the inhabitants of Gadara who "begged him to leave" (Mt 8:34). But others edified even Jesus, such as the Roman centurion whose faith exceeded anything Jesus has encountered among his own people (Mt 8:10), provoking him to threaten many of the chosen people with the dire consequences of faithlessness (Mt 8:11–13). Yet Jesus did not by any means neglect the people of Israel. In fact, the writer of Matthew's Gospel even suggests that the Twelve were explicitly ordered to avoid pagan territory and Samaritan towns (Mt 10:5) in order to concentrate exclusively on the Chosen People. But that is, literally, another story.

In going to the Jews, however, Jesus was by no means uncritical; nor was he impartial. He compared his own people to petulant children (Mt 11:16), was unable to do any miracles because of their lack of faith (Mt 13:58), and to their face called some of the Pharisees hypocrites (Mt 15:7), warning the people not to follow their lead (Mt 23:1-3). Jesus made no attempt to hide his partiality, exclaiming, "I thank you, Father, Lord of heaven and of earth, because you have hidden these things from the wise and the intelligent and have revealed them to infants" (Mt 11:25). As for the children—nonparticipant insiders—in a typical reversal (the first shall be last, masters shall be servants), Jesus referred to them as "the greatest in the kingdom of heaven" and challenged the disciples to "change, and become like little children,"[59] lest they be excluded from the kingdom. And for emphasis, when the disciples tried to turn children away, Jesus said: "Let the little children come to me, and do not stop them; for it is to such as these that the kingdom of heaven belongs" (Mt 19:15).

His partiality was not limited to children but extended quite deliberately to include every person or class excluded by the religious or political status quo—but was extended especially women, who were among his most steadfast and faithful followers. Some of them were indeed "sinners," but so indeed were many of the men, for as he said, "I have come to call not the righteous but sinners" (Mt 9:13). This is partiality at its most blatant. In contemporary language, this partiality was "the preferential option for the poor" and sinners; it lay at the very root of the liberating mission of Jesus.

Despite his unquestionable preference for those who littered the margins of society, Jesus was also an example of God's justice. Given the warnings he uttered and the reversals he promised and urged, he nevertheless focused part of his ministry on the participant insiders—those who exercised authority and wielded power. But unlike the invitations and forgiveness he tendered to the nonparticipants, he issued challenges and dire warnings to the participant insiders. They were the rich and powerful, those seated comfortably, the complacent. Jesus was a presence set to disturb and challenge them in no uncertain terms.

He warned them repeatedly that there was no safety and no hope for them if they remained at the center. Only if they turned their lives inside out by repentance and outreach, by reversal and service, would they have a chance—exactly the same chance as he offered to those who were on the edges and in servitude. It would be much harder, however, for "the rich" to enter the kingdom of God due to their own resistance, for they had too much to lose. "The poor," on the contrary, had little or nothing to lose and everything to gain. So it is that the kingdom of God is open to all, but is likely to be disproportionately represented by the marginal and forgotten members of society: "After all, God's primary election [and Jesus'] is not the church but the poor."[60]

Thus Jesus launches his two-pronged initiative to the insiders (fig. 6). First is his preferential option for the "nobodies," the "insignificant," "the last," on whose behalf he spoke so unequivocally. Then—simultaneously in fact—his initiative is to the "Number Ones." When, at the very beginning of his public life, Peter appears to want to act as an entrepreneur or agent for Jesus, Jesus immediately counters that his work is to keep moving, extending, inviting, and including all over Galilee (cf Mk 1:36).

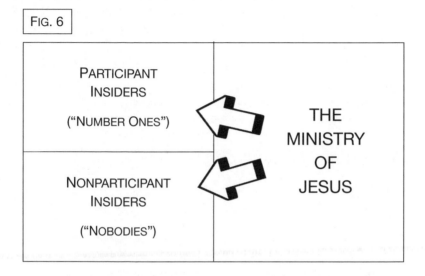

FIG. 6

PARTICIPANT
INSIDERS

("NUMBER ONES")

NONPARTICIPANT
INSIDERS

("NOBODIES")

THE
MINISTRY
OF
JESUS

Every society in recorded history is either unequivocally patriarchal or certainly biased in that direction. We may speculate about archaic matriarchy[61] and be impressed by societies at peace;[62] but patriarchy is the besetting sin of civilization—of settled human existence. As such, it is men who wield and covet authority, and since men have greater crude physical resources than women, they can turn such resources into social capital (authority), thus maintaining their dominance and control. As can be seen from the first quadrant in figure 5 (p. 106), adult males are virtually the exclusive source of authority.[63] Among the participant insiders, we can identify *significant others* (parents and other sources of moral authority), *legitimators* (disciplinarians and other sources of legal/juridical authority),[64] and individuals who exercise a combination of moral and legal authority. Typically, participant insiders or holders of authority are heads of households, members of the professions, and appointed or elected leaders, including those with specific legal, religious, or military jurisdiction. Women are not among them. All in all, such insider participants—as the name suggests—are responsible for and have control over the running of society. Not surprisingly, they are concerned with maintaining their authority, sometimes by an abuse of their power. They may consider themselves, or may be referred to, as "Number Ones," or "The Firsts," "VIPs"—or in some contexts, "Big Shots" (fig. 6).

By contrast, all other members of the society are nonparticipants (whether permanently or temporarily) in the sense that they may serve or service the society or community, but they do not have executive authority or the power of sanctions.

THE PREFERENTIAL OPTION OF JESUS

The most significant of the nonparticipants, both numerically and because they are not simply absorbed into the categories labeled "deviant" or "immature"[65] are women.

An obvious characteristic of human culture is what is commonly referred to as the sexual division of labor. Certain tasks and responsibilities typically belong to or are undertaken by men or women, respectively. Though everywhere there is some matching of responsibilities with sex-roles, such roles may vary crossculturally and may even overlap.[66] Thus women are typically responsible for child-rearing, but men are not always and everywhere irresponsible parents. Men are typically responsible for "breadwinning," but women are not everywhere uninvolved with agriculture or fishing. So much for role-distribution. But much more significant for our discussion is status.

Status, or the legitimate playing-out of a role or roles, may be achieved or acquired. An example of the first case is this: the child of illiterate parents may become an academic, thus achieving professorial status. In the second case, the legitimate offspring of royalty becomes royal simply by birth: this is acquired or inherited status and requires no special striving or achievement.

Women achieve the status of mother by giving birth. (That is not, of course, to say that role of mother is high status.) Other statuses may likewise be achieved. Yet particular societies will either limit the statuses available to women, or women's statuses will be deemed less significant than those of men. Thus in modern society, a woman teacher may have graduated in the same class as men yet her social position may remain inferior. In every single society there is some disparity between women and men: women are not acknowledged as men's equal. What God joined together, man—in this case, patriarchal males—has in fact divided. Some societies pride themselves on their treatment of women, while others are committed to maintaining male control. Even in the former, the view from women's perspective is never what it appears to men. And in the latter case, there is sometimes an explicit appeal to theology as the ultimate endorsement of inequality.[67]

In the time of Jesus, not only were women excluded from the executive positions (occupied by insider participants), but they were clearly and permanently nonparticipants; and in the Jewish patriarchal order their low status was rationalized and justified as being God's will. Jesus came to challenge and oppose this religious arrogance.

Nor was it only women who were classified as nonparticipants. Others lacking authority and social identity included the immature and the deviant (see fig. 5 on p. 106). The immature could, of course, grow up to become mature adults. If they did so—providing they were neither deviant nor women—they could be assimilated into the ranks of the participant insiders as respectable figures of authority and status. Still, the overwhelming majority of women had effectively no opportunity for social advancement.

Three categories of immature persons can be identified: the unborn, infants, and children. As a crosscultural exercise, it is illuminating to attempt to apply the biblical criteria for humanness (made in God's image, male and female, good, equal) and to examine how these particular categories are treated.

Every human community has to address the status of the unborn, the living, and the dead. The living must determine their responsibility both for the weak and the elderly who will soon die, and for the next generation still to be born. The moral capital of any community can be computed in terms of its attitude to these two vulnerable groups. The unborn need to be protected, and the sick and dying need to be nurtured. The only example of the unborn in the New Testament is the example of the pregnant Mary and her pregnant cousin Elizabeth (though the social significance of these pregnancies and of the mothers of the unborn Jesus and John is quite clearly enormous). But examples of the sick, dying, and even the dead, abound—from Peter's mother-in-law to Jesus' friend Lazarus, by way of the daughter of Jairus (Mt 9:18ff) to the daughter of the Caananite woman (Mt 15:21ff). These latter two examples not only show Jesus' preferential option for women in general, but specifically for the daughter of privilege (Jairus is an official) and for the daughter of an outcast (the Caananite women). Jesus treated people as specific, and as equal.

Infants and children are the other two classes of immature persons: the former lack language symbolically, as well as in fact they have nothing to say to the community, and the latter lack sexual identity (they have nothing yet to contribute to it). Speech will come, as will sexual maturity, and then the individuals will have something to offer. Meanwhile, such people are vulnerable and even dispensable in societies with high infant-mortality rates. Though, in the long term, the immature are critical to the well-being of the community, they are also relatively unproductive until they reach social adulthood. They may actually be exploited and are sometimes treated as less than human. But Jesus was always a defender of such persons, and his God's-eye view was that participant insiders were not morally superior to other people.

Finally, we consider the deviant. Every human society draws lines of separation and division, often with good cause. Without such discrimination, chaos would ensue. Law and order demands that there be certain treatment and sanctions for those who do not conform to what is deemed normal. Yet every human society is also imperfect, and none is above the disturbing presence and challenge of Jesus: a challenge to act justly, to love tenderly, and to walk humbly with God. We can distinguish three categories of deviant: physical, mental, and moral.

It may not be politically correct to speak of "deviants," but it makes an important point: human beings *are* labeled and treated with discrimination; and such discrimination is often justified by appeal to moral and legal principles. Thus, those considered physically deviant might include anyone who does not meet a particular societal norm: they are thus abnormal. The sick or aged, the paralyzed or crippled, deformed persons or amputees—some or all of these might be treated differently from those deemed normal. Then particular treatment, whether instutionalization, avoidance, punishment, or negative discrimination is legitimized. The same holds for those considered mentally deviant: from people with minor disabilities to those who are uncontrollable, from those classed as bipolar to those considered possessed.[68] Finally, we must mention those judged to be morally deviant. These would include convicted criminals or sinners in general: the former judged by legal criteria, and the latter by religious. But society judges not only those convicted but also those suspected of, or seen to be, acting in disapproved ways: prostitutes, moneylenders, those who exploit children, and others.

Here, then, are the nonparticipant insiders, the nobodies. They do include large numbers of nameless, faceless, and invisible males. But the categories of "immature," "deviant," and "women" are sometimes easier to spot. Of these—all nonparticipant insiders[69]— is the realm of God. To them does Jesus make his way.

THE DISTURBING MISSION OF JESUS

"What God has joined together, let no one separate" (Mt 19:6). Cultural man (including some women) will always be at odds with this injunction by virtue of cultural constraints and human perversity. No matter what culture Jesus might have encountered, and no matter what time in history the Incarnation might have occurred, Jesus would have found it necessary to issue a call to repentance, a return to what God intended. For despite magnificent cultural achievements, no culture is ever quite what God had in mind. There was always going to be conflict and confrontation between the message of Jesus and the culture(s) he encountered. As Gil Bailie pointed out, "In both life and death, Jesus was opposed by the most respected institutions of his world. The prospect of institutionalizing either the Sermon on the Mount or the revelation on the Cross are—not surprisingly—not great."[70]

It was not only in first-century Palestine that adult males wielded most of the power and authority; it has always been so. It was not only in his own society that women and children, the weak and the elderly—and many men—suffered discrimination; it has always been so. But Jesus wanted to show that it was not always *necessarily* so. He had a God's-eye view of the world, a view of the way things could be and should be if people would rethink their relationship with God. Of course, any success Jesus might have had would depend on the receptivity and the faith of those who heard him. Self-interest and self-righteousness, however, were always going to keep some from hearing the message and changing their minds. To change our minds is so very difficult for all of us.

So, from a position on the edge or at the margin of the lives of respectable people (lawyers, Pharisees, scribes, priests, rabbis, and the rest), Jesus attracted to himself and addressed his message precisely and explicitly to the nonparticipant insiders or the insignificant: "the last." Throughout his public ministry and preaching, we see how he encountered the physically sick, including blind or deaf people, lepers, and even dead people. We are amazed at his treatment of the mentally ill, including men, women, and even children in distress, as well as those believed to be possessed by demons. We are perhaps most astonished at his relationship with the morally deviant: criminals and quislings, adulterers and prostitutes, but also the contaminated and the ritually impure, from tax collectors to menstruating women. All these—and all women in particular—were among "the poor" who not only lacked authority or social status and had no prospects of achieving any, but who were told by the religious authorities that this was the way God had ordained the world.

Jesus came to expose the lie that God had favorites and that some people were hopeless cases to be permanently excluded from relationship with God. Jesus came to undermine religious assumptions and reverse the cultural flow: God did *not* endorse the exclusion of people and the sundering of society in the name of the maintenance of law and order and of the creation of spurious and arrogant theology. Jesus declared that in the realm of God, which he was initiating there and then, and which was to be in some considerable contrast to the reality of contemporary Jewish life, things would be very different. These very people, "the last," would in fact be first: children would receive revelation, women would be indispensable ministers, the blind would see, the deaf would dance, and the dumb would shout for joy. But there was more: those who were currently "the first" would, in fact, be last, masters would become servants, the self-righteous would be condemned, the exalted would be humbled, glut would turn to hunger, laughter to tears, and riches to impoverishment. To many who heard this message, this was good news indeed. But the very same words were anything but good news to the insider participants to whom Jesus also delivered the message.

Because the promise of the realm of God extended to everyone without exception—since Jesus came to erase the boundaries between people and to invite everyone equally—Jesus could not but address religious and legal authorities, and all those who enjoyed the status of significant other or legitimator. Though he could say "woe to you," he would also give them a choice, saying "unless you change"—for even the self-important were not beyond God's loving mercy. The rich, the complacent, the self-satisfied and the hypocrites can never enter the realm of God: but they can, in principle, change and be counted among the elect, though it is easier for a camel to pass through a needle's eye than for a rich person to reform. The rich are having their consolation now.

At the control center of every society, a group of privileged adult males wields authority over the social institutions and exercises the sanctions that maintain the social system. In so doing, the group is most likely to support the status quo and to maintain its own privileged position. This circumstance always means that some other people are used, exploited, or prevented from having equal rights, dignity, and freedom. There is always, in other words, an effective boundary that separates people. To the degree that participant insiders cling to authority and privilege and continue to occupy positions close to the center of power, to that degree they exclude themselves from the realm of God. But to the degree that they empty themselves, move to the edges or boundaries, encountering those from whom they are otherwise separated, to that degree they are already close to the realm of God where no lines of division and no zones of exclusion exist.

In human society there will always, of necessity, be both men and women. Likewise, there will always be national distinctions ("Jews and Greeks"). There will always be social statuses ("slave and free").[71] But in the realm of God and the community that Jesus preached, such biological, social, and religious distinctions, as well as other distinguishing characteristics between human beings across the face of the earth, will have no moral significance: all are one in Jesus Christ (Gal 3:26–9; Col 3:11). To some people, this is very good news, just as to others it is intolerable.

SUMMARY

Culture is critically important for understanding how reality is constructed and maintained; but it is sometimes understood either in a very superficial or in a rather romanticized way. We have been looking at the cultural context within which Jesus undertook his ministry. First, we examined the Genesis story, and then we looked at the effects of the "cultural flaw": separation and inclusion, and the cultural creation of "us" and "them." By looking at the activity of Jesus and the promise of Christianity (Gal 3: 26–29), we attempted to characterize the pastoral approach of Jesus and to indicate how far radical Christianity still has to go in order to be faithful to its calling. This examination should have demonstrated the importance of our making choices consistent with the preferential option of Jesus. As Christians, we have to act on the world rather than to acquiesce in the cultural reality in which we find ourselves. If we have been appropriately disturbed by the memory of Jesus, we will have a hunger and thirst for justice that will stimulate us to disturb the status quo in the name of the realm of God. Perhaps, then, we will become capable of more fully embodying authentic discipleship. In the next chapter, we identify some of the characteristics of such discipleship.

CHAPTER SIX

Mentors and Midwives, Images of Discipleship

SUSTAINERS OF COMMUNITY: MODELS OF DISCIPLESHIP

Meaninglessness" is an ugly word, but it is also a significant one. In fact, Viktor Frankl identified meaninglessness as the malaise of the twentieth century. We have been following his suggestions for crafting a more meaningful life, leaning also on Wordsworth's powerful image of "a presence that disturbs" as way of understanding God's presence and our response. Frankl's triple suggestion—that a meaningful life requires that we choose, encounter, and suffer—has shaped Chapter 4 (life through choosing) and Chapter 5 (love through encounter), and will provide a thread for this chapter (growth through suffering).

Christian discipleship entails the embrace of the Cross. We sign ourselves with the Cross of Jesus, and we bless one another with this sign of contradiction. As we hope for resurrection we also know that we too must proceed by way of the cross. How this becomes part of each disciple's life will, of course, vary. But we believe that our sufferings can be a way of encounter with a God who encourages and sustains. God disturbs us, too, but not perversely, for God is calling us to life. Yet life and growth are inseparable from suffering. If we accept the pain that we cannot change, along with a degree of bravery and some solidarity with those who offer support and encouragement, then we can actually grow in moral stature and discover that our lives are significant to those who love us. The meaning of life is not only to be sought within but beyond ourselves—a conviction shared by Viktor Frankl. The corollary is that when we stand side by side with those who suffer, we help to make their suffering bearable and to convince them that they are loved. Those who have suffered much are often the most compassionate; but the presence of a sustaining community can make all the difference.

As we continue to look, in this chapter, at the call to faithful discipleship, we consider two models of wise, nurturing, and life-giving encouragement. Mentors and midwives can sustain communities and bring out the most noble in individuals. Mentors and midwives can also be an inspiration: they can breathe the Spirit as they make their godly contribution to the community.

SEEKING WISDOM

It may help if we make explicit a number of assumptions before discussing our two heroic figures or ideal types. These assumptions will illuminate certain aspects of our Christian responsibility. Our focus is not explicitly on Christian saints, and we turn, perhaps, in an unexpected direction as we search for wisdom and encouragement.

The first assumption is, of course, that we have indeed felt something like the *disturbing* presence of God. It is not that we are strangers to God's *consoling* presence, but that we have been challenged in our complacency and we have been shaken out of our relatively comfortable lives by the God who calls and commissions us. The second assumption is that in consequence of *our developing relationship with God*, we are attempting—simply but seriously, and with due modesty and humility—to discover the fullness of life which Jesus promised (Jn 10:10). The third assumption is that we are not trying—or actually trying *not*—to be vainglorious or self-important but simply to be people of integrity and disciples of Jesus.

Given those assumptions—surely reasonable if we take God and ourselves with due seriousness—we are still required to face the social dimension of our faith and discipleship. Many Christians seem to overlook a crucial aspect of their baptismal responsibility: the duty to proclaim the Good News. But there is no escape, for baptism is designed to implicate us in the restoration of all things in Christ. We are called to encourage other people, first to become aware of the intrinsic power and the life-giving contribution of the Good News to their own lives, and then to encourage them to share with others the hope they themselves have experienced. It is not a matter of our trying to impress people, much less to proselytize them. Those who seek to impress place far too much emphasis on themselves, and those who presume to proselytize are invariably rude, even if they do not use force or fear. But good news, like less reputable forms of gossip, looks to spread itself; and by baptism we are commissioned to be bearers of Good News. To paraphrase Gustavo Gutiérrez, we are called to convince the poor that God loves them: not by honeyed words but by loving encounters. We are called to change the world: not by our own resources but by the power of God embodied in us.

There are countless good people: people of principle, people of justice, moral people, people committed to others. It would be patronizing to call them "anonymous Christians," and indeed it might be quite inappropriate to do so, especially if they are committed to a religion or practice that is quite clearly *not* Christian. Yet there are, among those countless good people, many who are perhaps "implicit Christians." Some of these may be *deliberately* implicit rather than deliberately explicit Christians, having been alienated from, or in some way scandalized by, institutional Christianity.

Many people experience Christianity as fatally compromised by its practices and practitioners, and as a travesty of its own good intentions and those of its founder. There are others, too, whose misplaced modesty allows them to consider themselves insignificant or irrelevant to the broader agenda of Christianity, which is the transformation of an unjust world and the restoration of human hope and dignity. The present chapter, therefore, will focus on the rather heavy responsibility that active, practicing Christians bear, for and toward those who have opted out of—or never opted into—Christianity.

It is often the case that the Christian faith, like the best and indeed the worst of human values, may often be, as we say, "caught, not taught." And it is universally the case that human beings are affected, for good or ill, by the example they see and the models they follow. If Jesus is an inspiration to those who follow him, the followers of Jesus should in turn be examples to others, for this is a requirement stipulated by Jesus himself (Jn 8:12; Mt 5:16).

This discussion brings us to a final assumption consistent with our theme: that those who have *felt* a godly presence that disturbs them should in turn *become* a godly presence that disturbs others. Just as we have been shaken out of our own inertia or false modesty by the God who calls and sends, so, as disciples and ministers [disciples are *"mathêtês,"* learners; ministers are *"therapeutês,"* attendants] we are called to cause others to stop, to notice, to ponder, and perhaps to turn and be converted to Christ. We are indeed our brothers' and sisters' keepers; but to remain faithful to our responsibility will always be onerous and is sometimes a measure of our own willingness to take up the cross.

MENTOR: GUIDE, MORAL SUPPORT

Homer's epic, the *Odyssey*, tells the tale of the departure of Odysseus from the rocky shores of Ithaca, bound for the siege of Troy and a lifetime's wanderings. With careful and explicit instructions, the king left his most trusted friend—Mentor by name—in charge of the royal household. This arrangement illustrates the *delegated model* of authority: authority is neither usurped nor clung to, but accepted as a responsibility and used on behalf of and for the building up of the community. Mentor was actually given full regal authority in the king's absence [Book 2:250]. He stood, therefore, not only *in loco parentis* but *in loco regis* and, in a certain profound sense, *in loco dei:* in the place of divinity. Notions of mentoring, and figures we call mentors, have become a part of our own lives, whether social or spiritual. Many of us have experience of mentoring or being mentored, or perhaps both. With this in mind, it might be profitable to revisit the original life and activity of Mentor. As persons disturbed by God, and as potential disturbers of others, we would do well to pursue our search for wisdom and illumination. The eponymous Mentor, to whom all other mentors owe inspiration, can be our guide.

Mentor appears at critical junctures throughout the *Odyssey*, always behaving courageously and impeccably. Perhaps the most interesting gift he receives—truly a gift of the gods—is this: he is endowed with the capacity actually to embody Zeus, chief among the gods, arbiter of moral order, protector of suppliants, punisher of the guilty. In a remarkable turn of the imagination, Homer's epic also chronicles a number of occasions when Mentor is even disguised as Athena, virgin daughter of Zeus, noblest of the female divinities, preeminent as a civic goddess and patron of wisdom in peace and war.

Our consideration of Mentor's experiences might take the form of a theological reflection on the place of mentoring in our own lives, and the presence of mentors—whether affirming or disturbing, and whether self-appointed or delegated by a higher power.

As an introduction, two general points should be made. First, Mentor enters the story as Odysseus begins his odyssey; immediately he evokes our sympathy and solidarity. At the same time, members of the household appear less sympathetic and loyal. "Out of sight, out of mind" is an apt description of the effect of Odysseus's departure; hardly has he left than the members of his household begin to show flagrant disregard for the king's intentions or Mentor's presence and advice. The stage is thus set for years of heartbreak, and the whole saga of the *Odyssey* is played out against a domestic background of this unrest. Just when Penelope (the wife of Odysseus) and Telemachus (his baby son) were most in need of support and a harmonious household, the very people who should have been promoting solidarity were fomenting dissent; and the moral authority of Odysseus was being undermined by those with no respect for him or for his lieutenant, Mentor.

From our vantage point as Christians and leaders, as bearers of some authority, and as, perhaps, even mentors ourselves, we can surely appreciate the tension and chaos that results from a failure or breakdown of appropriate mentoring. Chaos is especially evident wherever a community has a certain right to expect greater things of those placed in authority but experiences weak or nonexistent leadership.

A second general point is that in the absence of Odysseus, the goddess Athena—pivotal to the well-being and ultimate fate of all the people—would often come disguised as Mentor. In this way, Mentor was able to take some credit for extraordinary deeds of power. Equally important, Homer was able to show that where there is honorable effort and godly aspirations divinity may not be very far from humanity, and that the best efforts of mere mortals may be divinely inspired and life-giving. These are useful lessons for everyone.

Homer was able to identify what today we might call the feminine face of God, or the female aspect of God, active in human experience and history. This is perhaps a timely reminder that more than a millennium before Jesus other people were able to contemplate the idea of a God who was not restricted by the conventional limitations of the human imagination. From our perspective, we might reflect on the myriad ways in which a tried-and-true mentor can model or even embody aspects of divinity for us.

When we come to the dramatic unfolding of the story of the *Odyssey*, we encounter Mentor again at a number of critical moments. Homer actually crafts his great poem in such a way as to persuade us that were it not for the presence and action of Mentor, the magnificent epic would never have come to a happy ending. Without explicitly making Mentor indispensable to the story, Homer makes us appreciate his status among the principal players in the list of *Dramatis Personae*. The same point might indeed be made in regard to appropriate mentors in our own lives.

THE MENTOR: A PRESENCE THAT AFFIRMS

As the *Odyssey* continues, Telemachus has now grown to be a young man and still his father, Odysseus, has not returned. The resolve of his mother, Penelope, seems to be weakening, and her suitors are becoming increasingly demanding of her affections. Telemachus is trying to pluck up courage to sail in search of his father in an attempt both to assert his maturity and to fan the embers of his mother's dying hopes for her husband's safety. Yet Telemachus is only a callow youth, still lacking a man's beard.

At this point, Mentor appears to the young man. More precisely, though the figure that appears to Telemachus *appears* to be Mentor, it is actually the goddess Athena in disguise. Telemachus's noble enterprise requires some extraordinary assistance, so the young man's highest aspirations are underwritten by divinity itself. But, on this occasion, the mouthpiece or spokesperson is apparently Mentor, who offers encouragement and transmits the message: "You'll lack neither courage nor sense, if your father's spirit courses through your veins. So how can your journey end in shipwreck or defeat? There's every hope that you will reach your goal" [2:300ff].

Here is an example of one of the most important contributions of any mentor: to encourage. To encourage is to provide a measure of vicarious courage to the fearful, to strengthen the fainthearted, to support flagging spirits, and to embolden the pusillanimous.

Sometimes, and sadly, those in positions of authority understand their primary responsibility as issuing warnings or words of discouragement, offering words of caution or restraint, attempting to put old heads on young shoulders, or feeding their charges' growing appetite for risk-taking with the bland diet of conformity. However well-intentioned and, at times, benign these cautionary efforts may seem, they are actually authoritarianism rather than honest mentoring at work. Such use of authority may succeed in domesticating a wild or youthfully creative spirit, or in clipping the wings of a fledgling flier. But Mentor is wiser and more noble than this: he is an inspiration to Telemachus, urging him on to great things, speaking of high adventure, ultimate endeavor, abiding hope, and eventual success. Telemachus does not lack convictions but simply lacks courage, and Mentor gives him the courage of his convictions. That example shows what it means to encourage someone. Mentor is released from having to do everything himself and enables—and ennobles—the inexperienced youth.

Mentor makes an important reference and connection, assuring Telemachus of success in his dangerous enterprise "if your father's spirit courses through your veins." The young man must not only be encouraged to go in search of his father but may need to be reminded that he is indeed his father's son. No one was more courageous than the legendary Odysseus.

The application to Christian mentors and their protégés should not be lost. We are all called to undertake challenging adventures and we, too, need a father's spirit coursing through our veins. In our case, however, it is God's own Spirit endowing us with courage, and mentors must not forget it or allow it to be forgotten by those they guide.

Apart from willingness to strive (with some assurance of support in that willingness), being imbued by the Spirit of God (with some direction as to how this might be achieved), and having a spirit of adventure (with some inspirational models in the background), still more is required. Those with youthful convictions yet without vast experience need, like Telemachus, to hope.

Hope is never to be confused with optimism. Optimism is a product of reason and an interpretation of available information; hope is non-rational or beyond reason's horizons and is the product of enduring trust. Telemachus has threefold trust: trust in his father's heroic capacity for survival; trust in Mentor's encouragement; and trust in his own integrity. This powerful combination is one to ponder for our own lives. We need hope, born of trust, much more than we need optimism, for we live in a world in which optimism may be quite inappropriate. After all, we need a God in whom we can trust and with whom we can establish an enduring relationship. We need mentors, too, for appropriate guidance and for the kind of encouragement without which the best qualities in ourselves might never be realized. Yet unless we have discovered an inner core that assures us humbly of our self-worth and unerringly of our call to transcendence, we might never think to set sail and never imagine we might change the world.

Mentor has not yet finished with Telemachus and his quest. Once again, the goddess Athena—more able than the aging Mentor to cover ground at high speed—comes to the young man's aid. Once again disguised as Mentor, whose identity and moral authority are well-known, she undertakes to find a suitable crew for Telemachus. Now, a goddess might be thought to be capable of press-ganging a crew or even of finding a perfect group of people perfectly able to assist Telemachus in his noble enterprise, yet we find ourselves surprised at how events unfold. Though the voyage is highly dangerous and time is of the essence, Mentor actually goes in search of volunteers; and within a very short time there is a full crew of willing, if untested, sailors assembled for this adventure. Wise Mentor knows that press-ganged hands do not make a crew; he also knows that any and all forms of persuasion and seduction are likely to be counterproductive as well. Mercenaries or men who want to be mollycoddled will never generate the spirit of adventure or camaraderie—the spirit of communitas—that is necessary to sustain a dangerous voyage and bring a ship back to home port.

CLOSER TO HOME

Other lessons are embedded in this story. First, compromise is not always appropriate; second, life should not be made too easy; and third, there will always be young and generous souls ready for daring, risky adventures. The restless human spirit will never be completely tamed, and further, mentors will always attract those generous souls. So if the daring, risky souls do not gather where we might like them to, then perhaps the mentors are not of the caliber to attract them, or perhaps they are not advertising sufficiently daring, risky adventures.

Our Christian communities today are deeply in need of generous-hearted men and women, because there is a pervading sense that something is wrong, that some countervailing force is at work creating an unstoppable hemorrhage that is killing communities. A lesson from Telemachus and Mentor may be ours for the learning: where there is clarity of purpose and where noble ventures are to be undertaken, where there are inspired mentors who, in turn, inspire and encourage, there will be volunteers willing to commit themselves to undertakings that promise neither comfort nor predictability but which capture the imagination and fill up the soul.

By the time Telemachus is launched on his own high adventure, things on the home front have rapidly deteriorated. His mother, Penelope, legendary in beauty and faithfulness, is pursued by arrogant and self-interested suitors, and her palace is besieged by their greed and wastefulness. Clearly, the suitors are directly responsible for the misery that has befallen the once-proud court of Odysseus. Mentor suddenly appears on the scene. But this is no cavalry swooping down the valley on the sound of a bugle, no deus ex machina wheeled on stage to redeem a hopeless situation. Far from belaboring the suitors, Mentor actually turns the full force of his criticism and judgment on the rank-and-file members of the household. They had done absolutely nothing as the situation deteriorated, letting it go from bad to worse. They had neither spoken up nor strategized, while a small group of suitors had proceeded to eat them out of house and home. So Mentor charges them, the insiders, the local community, with bringing chaos upon themselves. He finds them guilty of sins of omission: they failed to do *anything*, when they could at least have done *something*. They could, says Mentor, have shown righteous indignation; they could have offered passive resistance; they could have behaved like human beings rather than like proverbial sheep.

The lessons here are profound. We may live in less-than-perfect situations, yet if we simply do nothing or if we wait for someone else—a person in charge, or perhaps even God—to perform a miracle and get us out of trouble, then we are failing to act in a fully human way. If we are complicit in unhealthy or unjust situations then our sins of omission condemn us. Mentor makes no bones about charging the householders as accessories to the crimes being committed under their own roof. Likewise, some of us— leaders, or people with responsibility within the Christian community—may be obliged to blame members of that very community, who fail to act in times of impending or actual chaos. It may, of course, be much easier to look outside or to find a hapless scapegoat, even though the realm of God seems so long in coming precisely because of the actions—or inaction—of the very people who profess most keenly to await it.

Mentor knows that his responsibility is no passport to comfort or the quiet life. In fact, he does not even content himself with criticizing the feckless household. He proceeds to turn his righteous indignation on the suitors. After all, they too are culpable, and Mentor is no respecter of persons. Mentor gives them the benefit of his scathing yet appropriate criticism, whereupon one of the chief culprits, in retaliation for Mentor's blunt speech, calls him an idiot to his face.

Those who are called to be mentors must have the courage to speak unpalatable truths, even though their courageous outspokenness and social conscience may be rewarded by contempt or vilification. There are always some who have no respect for mentors, just as there are always a need for mentors with courage and integrity, but the possibility always exists that mentors may be cowed by loud opposition, and always the chance that they may desert the post to which duty and godliness have called them.

As the story unfolds further Telemachus and his volunteers are now launched on the adventure of their lives. The young man is not only without experience on the high seas but has never commanded any group of people. Mentor once again instills confidence in his young charge. With his assistance, Telemachus issues his first commands to his crew who carry them out in exemplary fashion. Soon afterwards, the ship makes landfall in the country of King Nestor. When, filled with trepidation, the young commander approaches the king, Mentor is once again there to reassure: "Some of the words you will find within yourself; the rest, some power will inspire you to say" [3:30]. It is clear that Mentor is a true educator: he has the capacity to strike the spark of creativity, in his eager and well-intentioned but immature protégé.

This particular example is surely one of the most striking illustrations of the moral power of a good mentor. Homer's choice of words is quite amazing, and perfectly capable of being applied just as they stand, to Christian spirituality: "Some of the words you will find within yourself; the rest, some power [God] will inspire you to say." These are not only evocative of words spoken by Jesus to his closest followers, but are almost identical in tenor: "Do not worry beforehand about what you are to say; but say whatever is given you at that time, for it is not you who speak, but the Holy Spirit" (Mk 13:11).

Homer's message is profound. A mentor will not try to put words into the mouth of another nor make the young too stiff or self-conscious but will urge and encourage. In that way, the idealism of youth is not tempered or allowed to wilt. Under the tutelage of a wise mentor the young will find their own voice and not simply read someone else's script; they will break new ground and not simply tread in someone else's footsteps. A measure of the mentor's stature is the nobility of spirit that nurtures creativity and rejoices in whatever it inspires. Mentors know that they do not need to make copies of themselves.

As the epic of the *Odyssey* draws to its conclusion, Telemachus is reunited with his father, and Odysseus is victorious over his enemies. But in the end it is Mentor who, like the conductor of a mighty symphony orchestra, has created the final harmony. Yet even that is not strictly true for, since peace and the cessation of strife is a godly achievement, it is actually Athena, in the guise of Mentor, who bears the prime responsibility for bringing closure to twenty years of bitter discord and mindless destruction.

So we conclude, noting that a good mentor is sensitive to friction and fission in communities, knowing both how and when to bring healing closure to animosity and lasting peace to former enemies. It is no easy task, but it is critically important if human communities are to survive their own growing pains and overcome their worst instincts. It can only be accomplished by mentors with both true wisdom and the humility to allow God to work through them. Saint Paul, mentor of Timothy, exemplifies the strong and resolute qualities of such a guide in a nuanced and lengthy passage (2 Tim 1:1ff). Such mentoring is extended to all fledgling Christians who are encouraged to "rekindle the gift of God that is within you through the laying on of my hands; for God did not give us a spirit of cowardice, but rather a spirit of power and love and of self-discipline" (2 Tim 1:6).

THE MIDWIFE: TRUSTED GUIDE, MORAL SUPPORT

It may seem odd to use a character from an ancient Greek epic as a role model for those disturbed by God and as a focus for theological reflection, but I hope it has served its purpose. There is less need of explanation for the next example of a role model offered so that we might better respond to the God who engages our lives and commissions us to interact creatively and sometimes painfully with the lives of others: to be a presence that disturbs. The role model is the midwife.

Midwifery has been a social role throughout recorded history and across cultures boundaries. Every human community has acknowledged its need for the skills and wisdom of midwives and has raised up practitioners upon whom the community can always rely, sometimes, as a matter of life or death.

The etymology of the English word "midwife" is interesting, indicating that a midwife—like a mentor—is not, in principle, gender-specific: the morpheme "mid-" is actually a long-extinct preposition meaning with"; and the morpheme "-wife" is a standardization of "*wif*," meaning *woman*. So, strictly, a midwife is a "with-woman" or a person who is present to a woman giving birth. If we have conceptualized this word as a "woman-with," then we have misunderstood its original meaning. A midwife is strictly "a person [not necessarily female] with the woman (mother)."

The social history of midwives is varied and complex, and certainly worthy of reflection.[72] We immediately note the paradox of midwives in patriarchal societies. In many cultures, medical matters and medical practitioners were held in very low esteem. Yet despite the near-universal inferiority of women's status, women's skills in the "women's business" of pregnancy, confinement, childbirth, and child-rearing were both pivotal and widely respected. In practice, midwives were normally women. Theirs were hands of great dexterity, and they literally held life in those hands. Given the role of women attendants at virtually every birth, they certainly had power of life and death: were they to crush the infant's head or simply to remove the baby from its mother, they could have instigated a social and cultural revolution against dominant patriarchy. The fact that we do not know of any historical occasion in which midwives employed the ultimate tactic of crushing the infant's head as a sanction against patriarchy is actually quite astonishing. When men have had such accessible power over life and death, they have hardly ever shown such restraint.

Part of the explanation of such midwifely moderation may perhaps be found in a biblical passage. At the beginning of the Book of Exodus we read about the impressive fertility of the family of Israel in Egypt:

> But the Israelites were fruitful and prolific; they multiplied and grew exceedingly strong, so that the land was filled with them. Now a new king arose over Egypt, who did not know Joseph. And he said to his people, "Look, the Israelite people are more numerous and more powerful than we. Come, let us deal shrewdly with them, or they will increase and, in the event of war, join our enemies and fight against us and escape from the land" (Ex 1:7–10).

So the Israelites were singled out for punitive treatment. But they continued to reproduce, and the Egyptians became even more afraid. Sanctions were tightened, and the lives of Israelites were made more even miserable. Still they grew in number:

> The king of Egypt said to the Hebrew midwives, one of whom was named Shiphrah and the other Puah, "When

you act as midwives to the Hebrew women, and see them on the birthstool, if it is a boy, kill him; but if it is a girl, then she shall live." But the midwives feared God; they did not do as the king of Egypt commanded them, but they let the boys live. So the king of Egypt summoned the midwives and said to them, "Why have you done this, and allowed the boys to live?" The midwives said to Pharaoh, "Because the Hebrew women are not like the Egyptian women; they are vigorous and give birth before the midwife comes to them." So God dealt well with the midwives; and the people multiplied and became very strong. And because the midwives feared God, he gave them families (Ex 1:15–21).

This story illustrates a number of points. First, it is unusual that two women—Shiphrah and Puah—are actually named in the biblical text. This naming is perhaps an indication of the significance both of their social role and of the fact that they and their deeds could be explicitly remembered by later generations. Second, if birth control is the issue here, then the king's strategy is rather misguided: it would be much more effective to kill the potential bearers of children than the potential begetters. Even a few surviving males could make many women pregnant, whereas a large number of males could not reproduce faster than the capacity of the surviving women. Furthermore, by killing the boys the king would deprive himself of the very workforce he had come to rely on.

The most interesting fact, however, is that the midwives, perhaps by a show of solidarity, actually succeeded in resisting the king. However afraid they might have been, they were committed to creativity and not to destruction, to bringing to birth and not to dealing death. The king now had to appeal to his own people to drown Israelite boy babies. If he had done that initially or if he had infiltrated the ranks of the pregnant Israelites, he might have had more success.

Midwives are present at the very moment of new birth and are committed to life itself. But they are also committed to supporting the birth mother. Part of their function in the Exodus story is to assist the birth mother to fulfill her own indispensable role. There is a reference to a midwife in the Book of Genesis, when Rachel is struggling with a difficult labor that will in fact take her life. The midwife does not save Rachel, but her consoling voice is there: "Do not fear; you will have this son." It echoes the very voice of God, "Do not be afraid," reiterated over and over again for anxious and troubled souls. Midwives are not miracle workers but they do offer indispensable moral support.

Midwifery is recorded in ancient India, and we know that in Greece and Rome midwives were respected and acknowledged as "professional" providers of care. The point is, of course, that human cultures and societies cannot manage without midwives.

SOCIAL HISTORY OF MIDWIVES

Traditionally, midwives learned by the *apprentice model,* becoming proficient by practice. Midwifery, in common with carpentry or other arts, crafts, and skills, is learned by doing, by active observation and gradual engagement under the tutelage of a respected practitioner. Such learning is informal and requires the building up of relationships of respect and trust. It is cumulative and, effectively, unending; it can only happen by long exposure to the discipline and to its practitioners. Though an essential part of the skill is amassed through imitation, that is never enough: the midwife needs both creativity and credibility, which cannot be learned. Yet the apprentice model is proven, effective, and well-adapted to encouraging the diffident and excluding the incompetent.

Skills and knowledge are passed down from generation to generation yet are not immutable. Studies of traditional societies show that the human community is adaptable and creative and even when its members are convinced that they have faithfully transmitted or loyally received the practical wisdom of their forebears, there are, nevertheless, always slight modifications. Consequently, over generations, amnesia or accretion (and perhaps both) may have imperceptibly changed the original deposit of tradition: this result, of course, is a sign of a living culture.

Between the high Renaissance and the Enlightenment (the seventeenth and eighteenth century), Europeans undertook a formalization of medical knowledge; the domination of the scientific method came to marginalize women in general and midwives in particular. As early as the first decades of the seventeenth century, enormous changes had already taken place. As more and more male physicians were formally trained, they quickly restructured and dominated the medical field, with the result that they themselves gravitated toward the more affluent and socially respectable sections of the community. Ironically, the traditional midwives had little choice but to serve the marginalized poor, immigrants, and the rural communities: in other words, the most needy and thus the most deserving. Accelerating this outreach was the fact that quite soon women midwives were refused access to hospitals and their women patients.[73] Midwives, therefore, made a virtue out of necessity, as they worked "on the edge." But as they did so, their own subculture produced innovations, largely in terms of supportive and empathetic attitudes. Meanwhile, men also dramatically improved birthing skills, particularly for difficult births, by inventing new tools. But they adamantly refused to share them with women. So perhaps it was that male expertise professionalized the science of obstetrics and located its practice outside the community in hospital institutions, while women's skills normalized the art of birthing and located its practice within the community in people's homes.

By the early twentieth century, the skills of midwives were widely practiced all over the world, each community or culture integrating its own birth attendants or wise women (in France, midwife is *sage femme*: wise woman) into the rhythms of its own life. The great social upheavals which saw the dramatic influx of Europeans into the United States also found different ethnic groups bringing, not only their own diet, beliefs, practices, and clergy, but their own midwives. Universally, the presence and influence of midwives has remained significant. Even in many countries where it was in temporary decline,[74] it has seen significant revival as communities have clung to their intuitions about birth.

Pregnancy and delivery are not sickness or aberration but a normal part of life. Thus they should be integrated into, rather than separated from, the community. It is estimated that in our own day, when approximately a quarter of a million babies are born *each day*, probably 140,000 of them begin their independent life in the safe, warm hands of a midwife. In the United States, most babies today are delivered in hospitals by obstetricians. In consequence, the number of midwives has declined. Nevertheless, midwife-assisted births continue to show a markedly lower perinatal mortality and require only 50 percent of hospital Caesarians. And even in the U. S., five thousand nurse-midwives attend an increasing number of births annually.[75]

MIDWIFE AS PARABLE

"Safe in her hands" depicts, as well as anything, the relationship between a newborn infant and a midwife. Let us use that image and explore some of its possibilities as we consider our Christian responsibility as analogous to that of the midwife, or our need as Christians for appropriate "wise women (or men)" to support and encourage our struggle toward life.

First, there is a remarkable overlap of connotations between mentors and midwives: both are committed to the life and well-being of others. Like Mentor who was God in disguise (sometimes quite literally) and charged with assuring the safety and survival of his charges, so a midwife carries awesome responsibility for the well-being both of those who give birth and of those who are brought into the world.

As assistant, facilitator, and birth attendant, the midwife may be seen as a kind of co-creator and life-deliverer in relation to the newborn child, and also as a minister to the new mother. The midwife cannot, of course, give birth herself, but is able to *bring to birth*; the midwife is not the mother, but is *needed* by the mother. In a fashion similar to a mentor, a midwife offers presence, experience, and moral support. Like a mentor, a midwife cannot replace those she serves but must be personally charged with integrity and capable of bringing out the best in others. As a mentor self-consciously stands in the place of a higher power and endeavors to act in a godly fashion, so a midwife holds the Creator of life in the highest regard and endeavors to be an appropriate instrument by which human life continues. Both mentors and midwives have learned how to be themselves and also how to subsist in the presence of the mystery of life. These are truly godly qualities.

Second, midwives have gifts that are unique and special, yet complementary to the capacities of the mother. The midwife simply cannot take over for the mother but must know how to encourage the mother and elicit her best efforts. The midwife must have extensive knowledge and experience of the process of birth and its potential complications but also the wisdom to determine when to intervene and when to wait, when to challenge and when to cajole. The midwife must, above all, be aware of the power of her personal presence and moral support, and she must never frighten, threaten, or trick those she attends.

Third, the midwife, like the mentor, occupies a social role that is crossculturally constructed. Both mentors and midwives are to be found universally, but the expression of their service varies from one culture to another. So it is worth pondering, first on the simple fact that different human communities set such store by mentors and midwives, and then on the fact that there might be subtle variations in the way they make their contribution in particular contexts. The more sensitively we resonate with the harmonies of various societies, the more we may discover ways of being relevant. At least we may minimize our intrusiveness in a globalized and multicultural world.

Finally, the midwife is not only an important link with the past and with tradition but also an agent for change. Experience shows that as new techniques relating to pregnancy, birth, and infancy become available, they will only be assimilated into communities if endorsed by local midwives. Midwives are the gatekeepers who oppose the entry of undesirable elements and who welcome acceptable change. Whether in rural Africa or contemporary North America, change does not only come from the top but is assimilated into the community by the community's most trusted agents, such as mentors and midwives.

Pastoral-Theological Applications

Can the notion of midwifing be of assistance to contemporary Christian communities, or to communities whose faith needs to be revitalized? Are there persons with courage and wisdom who may have the expertise and moral authority to support those who are fearful and to bring out the best in those without whom the future of our communities will be compromised, perhaps mortally? Are there people in our communities who have a vital contribution to make, even to a society that may fail to appreciate them?

Many of us live in societies in which the components of wisdom—knowledge and experience—seem to have become separated. In the age of the Internet, knowledge is commoditized and easily available. As for experience: it may simply accrue, like a steady buildup of dust, to those whose life-expectancy is up to 70 percent greater than that of their forebears a century ago. But knowledge is not always internalized and applied, and experience does not inevitably bear fruit (we may recall T. S. Eliot's "we had the experience but missed the meaning"). If wisdom is the fruit of knowledge and experience, many lives would seem to be barren. When a sense of futility, meaninglessness, or sheer despair marks the lives of so many, it is not surprising that they fail to bear fruit. Everyone is then impoverished.

Is our society (wherever we are) able to learn by its mistakes? Do our communities (whatever they are) use their experience to modify their behavior? Do some of us (whoever we are) even pursue knowledge as the accumulated wisdom of previous generations, or do we only aspire to be purveyors of trivia or repositories of factoids?

Those who claim not simply to believe in Jesus but actually to have a relationship with and experience the Risen Christ in their lives, bear a large responsibility for midwifing life in people and communities who are struggling for viability in the contemporary world. We who consider ourselves people of faith have a social duty to a world looking for encouragement, moral support, and a degree of authority that is not authoritarian. Religion is never simply a private matter, and faith is not merely a claim to a privileged relationship with God. Our lives are stunted unless they are lived for others: the disciples of Jesus are to be salt of the earth and light of the world (cf. Mt 5:13–16).

In the lives of mature and serious Christians, willingness to be of service to the wider community should be paramount. More specifically, there should be room for the exercise of some of the skills of midwives primarily because the community needs assistance, and because such Christians have resources that properly belong to the community.[76]

But a countercurrent runs through many of our communities, especially in the rich nations of the contemporary world. There is, currently, in the United States, a reaction against integrated, natural childbirth programs offered by midwives. A recent study determined that many people "perceive the holism of the home-birthers...as frightening, irresponsible, limiting and disempowering. While home-birthers see the hospitals as out-of-control technology running wild over women's bodies, professionals experience the hospital and its technology as a liberation from the tyranny of biology, and as empowering them to stay in control of an out-of-control biological experience. As the babies birthed [in hospitals] are carried off to the nursery and placed in their separate bassinets, and spend much of infancy in their separate cribs and plastic carriers, so in later years they will be carried off to daycare and to school. *Ours is a nation founded on principles of separation.*"[77] The emphasis is mine; the ongoing responsibility belongs to us all.

Finally, lest we too hastily identify midwives with women—and allow men prematurely to absolve themselves of co-responsibility—we might pursue a theological reflection by referring to an extraordinary passage in Plato's *Dialogues*. Socrates is speaking:

Have you never heard that I am the son of a midwife, brave and burly, whose name was Phaenarete? I myself practice midwifery. Bear in mind the whole business of the midwives and then you will see my meaning better. It is said that Artemis was responsible for [determining the rules for midwives]. Though she is the goddess of child-birth, she is not herself a mother. She could not allow the barren to become midwives because human nature can-not know the mystery of an art without experience; but she assigned this office to those who are too old to bear, honoring their resemblance to herself. Such are the mid-wives, whose task is a very important one, but not so important as mine.

My art of midwifery is in most respects like theirs; but differs, in that I attend men and not women, and I look after their souls when they are in labor, and not after their bodies: and the triumph of my art is in thoroughly examin-ing whether the thought which the mind of the young man brings forth is a false idol or a noble and true birth.[78]

There are a number of significant points here. First, says Socrates, "the barren [cannot] become midwives." Yet our own experience shows that those who have not borne children of their own are not always "barren": just as those who actually give birth are not always life-giving or the best of parents. Socrates himself is the exception that proves the rule that he is articulating.

Second, "the triumph of [the] art [of midwifery] is in thor-oughly examining whether [what is born] is a false idol or a noble and true birth." This evokes another Socratic saying, "the un-examined life is not worth living," and reminds us of our need for those who will help interpret and assess our own lives.

Third, Plato (like his younger contemporary Aristotle and unlike Emmanuel Kant two millennia later)[79] obviously knew the importance of role models: he insisted that people learn virtue by being affected by virtuous people rather than by learning abstract notions. It's an observation that has sometimes been lost sight of, but which every true mentor or midwife embodies and every nov-ice needs to experience.

It would do no harm at all if we were to ask what, apart from obvious biological and gender similarities, makes women, in par-ticular, good midwives. Why, apart from the obvious consider-ations, is the role thought to be inappropriate for most men? Can men learn anything from women's dedicated presence to, and support of new life? Betty Friedan has written persuasively about "crossover,"[80] when persons begin to express the integration of their masculine and feminine sides, when competitiveness gives way to collaboration, and when a hidden dimension of humanness appears. "In reclaiming and integrating their suppressed masculine and feminine sides, these elders play a larger parental role that helps to keep the whole tribe human, and the species to survive" (Friedan, p. 86). Is this not expressed in the art and wisdom of mentoring as in midwifing? So mentors can learn midwives' wisdom, midwives can capture mentors' dignity, and God's spirit—present in the best of each—can bring new life to birth and renew the Christian community.

SUMMARY

This chapter has offered a pair of images as a spur to a reflection on the social dimensions of radical discipleship. Mentors and midwives serve the community and not their own interests; but it is their probity and integrity, as much as their undoubted skill, that gives them credibility. They model what they teach, they help form minds, and they instill resolve into timid hearts. They embody the axiom that to love we must encounter. They illustrate something we saw in the survivors of the holocaust: the importance of tradition and its transmission. As people aspiring to continue as radical Christians in a world that has largely lost its taste for Christianity, we may take some comfort from the inspiration of Mentor and the figure of the midwife, and in turn hope to distill and transmit some of the qualities embodied in their lives. Mentor was a disturbing presence but not officious or self-important. Midwives may have to disturb the lives of those to whom they minister but theirs is a life-giving disturbance. In each case, these figures of people who contribute to the common good have first been touched or inspired by divinity, by the Creator, by God. Neither mentors nor midwives are quick to seek power or influence; but when called by, from, and for the community, they do not shrink from the challenge.

CHAPTER SEVEN

Strangers in the Spirit of Jesus

A PRESENCE THAT DISTURBS

A presence that disturbs" is the title and topic of this book, and we have considered a number of implications of the phrase. One implication, though, deserves special attention: the disturbing presence of the stranger. But the stranger I have in mind here is not raucous—yet relevant, and not central—yet significant.

We are all familiar with being surprised, or even shocked, by a strange person or someone we consider a stranger. We may also acknowledge that we are prejudiced against other people in certain circumstances. Perhaps assisted by some of the reflections about the disturbing ministry of Jesus,[81] we may be quite conscious of the cultural tendency to separate and divide by creating categories. If so, we will be aware that those we call strangers are those we ourselves put into a culturally constructed category. Strangers, we might say, are not born but made.

The word "stranger" really belongs with its other half, for it is one of a pair. The paired term is usually thought of as "host," but perhaps that is not the most useful paired term. The paired term can only be arrived at by looking at particular cases and contexts.

Essentially, the word "stranger" is really only defined in relation to another term, which is why relations with strangers and, particularly, the stranger's relation with others can be so ambiguous.

The term "xenophobia" means, strictly speaking, *fear of the stranger*. More broadly, it means lack of respect, intolerance, or distaste for the stranger, though it may indeed refer to real hatred. The person lacking in respect or showing intolerance is, of course, the self-defined insider or nonstranger. Xenophobia can only operate where a line of distinction and division has been drawn between persons. But it is also possible to draw lines between people for rather less ignoble reasons: xenophilia or philoxenia are the more attractive faces of outreach to strangers. The words themselves are much less common than xenophobia (a fact that is interesting in itself: perhaps we don't sufficiently practice what these words point to). They speak of active respect for, and kindness to, strangers. The Good Samaritan is a fine example of xenophilia or philoxenia. However, philoxenia was inculcated as a virtue long before Christianity.

In the *Odyssey*, Homer notes on several occasions that hospitality to the stranger is one of the most important human characteristics and a measure of society's moral health. Zeus often comes disguised as a stranger in order to check on people's virtue in this regard. Therefore, whoever encounters a stranger should either instinctively respond with authentic hospitality, or—less nobly—at least be aware that the stranger could be Zeus in disguise. Jesus, of course, said something very similar indeed: "I was a stranger and you welcomed me" (Mt 25:35).

The stranger, then, is someone seen *from another person's perspective*. People do not think of themselves primarily as strangers, since most people most of the time are at home or are insiders, whereas the stranger is someone not at home or not an insider. People are thus called "stranger" and treated accordingly by those who themselves are at home or who are insiders. The insiders perceive themselves to be in charge and legitimately able to take initiatives that are not open to the stranger. The stranger is, in a rather literal sense, *defined* by the other: boundaries are set by the other, and the stranger is expected to respect those boundaries and operate within them.

Not only is the stranger not self-defined, the stranger is not even self-sufficient. An obvious characteristic of the stranger is that he or she is *out of place:* and not only out of place but out of knowledge, resources, shelter, and perhaps safety too. The stranger is thus needy and dependent, to some degree, on other people and their knowledge, resources, and shelter, and perhaps on the safety they can offer. (The obvious fact that not all strangers accept a measure of dependence, and that some are aggressors, will also concern us later.)

To be neither self-defined nor self-sufficient is highly problematic for many people, and not totally comfortable for anyone. Some people try to resolve the problem by assertiveness or worse, while others know that they must learn a new social language: when out of one's own place and in another's place, one must develop new skills, behaviors, and responses. Yet the stranger is in no position to know exactly what is expected or required and, therefore, is likely to make mistakes and feel ignorant and vulnerable. Again, no one finds the role of a stranger comfortable, but some are more gracious than others as they adapt to this role.

Self-definition, in some form, is a human characteristic: either we imagine ourselves as self-made people (creators of our own unique identity and *persona*), or we decide how much of other people's definitions of ourselves we will accept. Perhaps there is an element of both these processes in all of us. But though not self-defined, the stranger does have some recourse: though primarily defined by others, the stranger may have the option of accepting, rejecting, or modifying the definitions of others and thus may enter into a kind of dialogue or negotiation.

Strangers who remain for some time *out of place* and in another's place must not reject the other's definition and expectations of them. To do so would be effectively to deprive themselves of a social identity, for the concept of stranger is not just a label, and every stranger is the bearer of an identity. Nonaggressive strangers are conventionally expected to accept the hospitality they receive. Better put, they have a choice: they are expected to choose to accept without undue protest whatever they are offered. Such acquiescence is not permanent but provisional; it serves to indicate that the stranger is now willing to be put *in his or her place* by another, *whose place this is*. From this place (which is now *a new place* for both stranger and host), a new social identity and relationship can, in time, be fashioned.

In many languages, a single word applies to both *stranger* and *guest*, echoing the injunctions of the *Odyssey* or the life of Jesus: strangers warrant gracious hospitality. But in the memories of many societies there is a darker side to the interaction with a stranger: the stranger is a potential threat, an enemy, a destroyer. Such memories create tension and ambivalence for communities who also rate hospitality among the highest human qualities: open hospitality may lead to destruction ("I fear the Greeks bearing gifts" [Virgil]). Nevertheless, lack of respect for genuine strangers marks one as less than human and may produce longstanding animosity. It is thus not surprising that some strangers feel somewhat uncomfortable and controlled: these feelings actually are the result of their being scrutinized and assessed prior to any firm commitment by their hosts.

When a *stranger* is treated as a *guest*, he or she will feel relatively at ease, since the conventional treatment of guests includes their being made to feel at ease or even *at home*. However, when the stranger is actually treated more like a *stranger*—as strange, alien, unknown, peculiar—then he or she will probably feel decidedly uncomfortable. When people feel uncomfortable, they are much more likely to want to change things than when they feel comfortable. But because the stranger is going to be treated as strange, even though he or she may also be treated temporarily to the status of a guest, the stranger will find it difficult to resist the desire to escape or at least to take control.

Social Conventions and Strangers

Encounters between a stranger and a host always take place where the host is, never where the stranger is. This is the nature of such encounters and of the social roles of the two parties. But not only is the host at home, the host is superordinate or "one-up" relative to the stranger, who is thus subordinate or "one-down."

When the stranger is actually being treated conventionally as a guest, the rules are different: the host defers to the guest and serves the guest as the guest's subordinate, while the guest in turn accepts preferential treatment and plays the superordinate role of the VIP. Nevertheless, it is still the host who is in charge, who has arranged everything, who has made executive decisions, and who has assumed responsibility for the occasion. The guest cannot linger indefinitely or take charge: convention demands that the guest "plays a part" as it were and acknowledges that the host is engaging in a little role reversal in order to honor the guest.

The host, then, is structurally superordinate, and the stranger/guest structurally subordinate. As long as both conform to the implicit rules, all will be well. But if the stranger/guest should try to take control, or indeed if the host should abdicate responsibility, the structure will begin to collapse.

Between stranger and host, there is unequal authority and an asymmetrical relationship. It is simply not possible for stranger and host to alternate statuses and roles in order to maintain equality. As long as one person is stranger and the other is host, the former must defer and the latter must take responsibility. The stranger is always dependent on the host in a way that is simply not true for the host in relation to the stranger. In fact, the relationship between the two actually depends on inequality. This relationship may require some reciprocity or mutuality, but it is not an equal relationship.

Some people have great difficulties, whether philosophical or social, with unequal relationships. They tend to equate unequal with invalid or unacceptable. However, the relationship between a parent and a young child, or indeed between ourselves and God, is surely unequal, yet valid and acceptable. But in social relationships between adults, some people are uncomfortable until they have leveled the playing field. The inability or unwillingness to be part of an unequal relationship greatly contributes to the breakdown of social life, and some who consider themselves democratic and egalitarian may be incapable of forging relationships outside their own culture until they are willing to learn new ways. If the stranger knows his or her place, and the host likewise, then matters may proceed very well, in *unequal mutuality*—an interesting notion indeed.

The stranger is, by definition, not only strange but ambiguous. The stranger represents or stands for both a welcome and a feared encounter, both promise and threat. As long as the stranger remains a stranger, ambiguity will be part of the stranger's social identity. For a particular person to want to resolve such ambiguity is quite understandable, but for the host community to allow the ambiguity to dissolve is to risk becoming dangerously complacent. The host need not impute ill will or bad faith to an individual stranger but does need to be vigilant. The stranger in turn needs to understand that the host's vigilance should not necessarily be taken too personally, but in order to be a successful stranger one must learn to live with ambiguity.

People raised in a dominant culture or in one of the rich and powerful nations of the world instinctively tend to think of themselves as "insiders"; it is others who are "outsiders." When other people (strangers) come to their shores, they (hosts) may be very hospitable and not notice the asymmetry of the relationship and the fact that they (hosts) hold power and initiative. However, when these "insiders" go abroad, even though they are in unfamiliar territory, they cling to their own "insider status" and the power and initiative that accompany it. Some of them are much less capable of dealing with the unexpected ambiguity and lack of power and initiative they experience, and some attempt to wrestle control from their potential hosts. The extreme example of this would be when people from a dominant culture, now living in someone else's world, actually think of the local inhabitants as strangers. This complete inversion of social reality characterizes the "ugly American" or indeed the "ugly outsider" of whatever persuasion.

In order to understand this propensity and learn how to address it, we can look at two contrasting social realities and their contrasting social requirements. I will identify the issues by means of a fictive first-person account:

When You Are the Stranger, I Am in Control
The story goes like this:

> You, the stranger, have come from somewhere else and
> have arrived at my place: I am at home, at the center of
> my familiar world. Therefore, I have higher status than
> you and can orchestrate the encounter. I do not know
> much about your own background and may not be very
> interested. But because I am a cultured and socially re-
> sponsible person, I will take care of you and indulge you,
> though not, of course, indefinitely. We have a proverb
> that says "on the first day, the stranger/guest smells sweet;
> on the second day the smell is getting stale; by the third
> day, the smell is like a dead fish."
>
> I am in control, and I will ask you polite questions
> about your background, though I do not expect long-
> winded and detailed answers. I do, however, expect you
> to appreciate what I offer you, and indeed what I possess,
> both materially and in terms of my personal status. I can
> afford to indulge you, but you should acknowledge my
> generosity. You don't need to worry about anything: I
> will look after you.
>
> Actually I feel a bit sorry for you. You don't seem to
> have much initiative, and some of the things you say are
> really quaint and odd. You are a bit strange. I'm glad I'm
> not you.

When I Am the Stranger, You Are in Control
In reverse circumstances, the story might read as follows:

> I, the stranger, have come from far away and I am tired.
> I am glad to be here with you, and though I would
> dearly like my privacy and freedom, I am truly grate-
> ful for your hospitality. Nevertheless, I will be glad to
> get home again. I really don't know what is expected
> of me, and I feel both useless and self-conscious. It's
> quite pleasant to be looked after, but I have no idea of

what will happen next, and I feel powerless to do anything about it.

You are very kind, and yet I find I am always trying to please you and to read your mind. I want to give you the answers that you seem to want, so I look for clues in the kinds of questions you ask. But this is rather enervating: I can't relax.

I have my own thoughts and patterns of behavior, but you don't seem to want to know about them. I always feel that I'm being scrutinized. Actually, I'm beginning to feel very resentful of you and all you have, and even of the relaxed way you sit there being kind to me. I feel you are sometimes just a poseur, and if I could get up and leave, I would. But I'm stuck here.

This reconstruction may identify some of the thoughts and feelings typical of the insider/host or the stranger/guest. It is important to acknowledge such thoughts and feelings not only as more or less confirming our own but as characterizing other people too. Then perhaps we—sensitive Christian disciples—can take comfort from the fact that our experience is not wildly unusual and also empathize with others who are experiencing some discomfort or unfamiliarity.

SWITCHING ROLES AND CHANGING STATUS

As in everything else, Jesus is our role model. His whole public ministry was marked by movement, by encounter, by role-switching and by role reversal. It is a tour de force on his part. But if we want to be the kinds of disciples we are called to be, then we must choose to follow Jesus, a choice that entails our learning from him.

The starting point—though Jesus is God and we are not—is the fundamental option of Jesus, expressed magnificently in the Letter to the Philippians. But we are not simply told about Jesus, we are bidden to *have the same mind and attitude* as he has. Here is the whole passage:

If then there is any encouragement in Christ, any consolation from love, any sharing in the Spirit, any compassion and sympathy, make my joy complete: be of the same mind, having the same love, being in full accord and of one mind. Do nothing from selfish ambition or conceit, but in humility regard others as better than yourselves. Let each of you look not to your own interests, but to the interests of others. Let the same mind be in you that was in Jesus Christ,

> who, though he was in the form of God,
>   did not regard equality with God
>   as something to be exploited,
> but emptied himself,
>   taking the form of a slave,
>   being born in human likeness.
> And being found in human form,
>   he humbled himself
> and became obedient to the
>   point of death—
>   even on a cross.
>
> Therefore God also highly exalted him
>   and gave him the name
>   that is above every name,
> so that at the name of Jesus
>   every knee should bend,
>   in heaven and on earth and
>   under the earth.
> and every tongue should confess
>   that Jesus Christ is Lord,
>   to the glory of God the Father.
>   PHILIPPIANS 2:1–11

So Jesus did not cling to his own status, but presented himself to humanity in a comprehensible fashion: in a way we human beings, in our own context and with our own limitations, could absorb and understand.

Nevertheless, Jesus also moved a great deal—and not only geographically. He moved from being an insider to being an outsider, from being one up to being one down, from the position of master to the position of servant, and from the role of host to the role of stranger. He also knew the difference between an honored guest and a simple stranger, and the nuances of being in each of these positions. We may have made a virtue of identifying *the other as stranger* and of treating the other accordingly, at the expense of acknowledging that sometimes *we are the stranger* and that we need to modify our behavior in order to respond appropriately to whatever demands that role makes on us. After all, however worthy it is to care for the other as stranger, such behavior would always leave us with the initiative—in control, superordinate, one up. But Jesus explicitly called for role reversal, for the first to be last and the master to be servant. Given that this requires not only good will but the yielding of initiative and control—and the acceptance of a subordinate, one-down status— this role reversal is much easier to talk about than to accomplish.

It is extremely difficult for anyone to negotiate both the position of stranger and that of host with integrity, but if proficiency in both roles can be achieved, it would have a number of virtues. It would prevent the buildup of oppressive asymmetrical relationships, it would neutralize internalized oppression in the other, it would mitigate unwholesome dependency, and it would create a community of equals. It would ensure that the pendulum would swing smoothly between the one up and the one down, between the superordinate and the subordinate. It would ensure that no one would either cling to power or become forever a vassal of another. Even contemplating such a prospect, however, requires that one be steadfastly committed to relationships of mutual enhancement. Actually to undertake such a prospect requires that one must have the spirit of Jesus himself.

How did Jesus approach such a challenge? As a host, he took initiatives, gathered people together, made them welcome and put them at ease, served them, and used his position to benefit them. In so doing, he restored identity and dignity to outcasts and to those who were overlooked or forgotten. As a stranger or guest, he showed himself as the kenotic one who emptied himself of status and dignity and who allowed other people to issue invitations, take initiatives, play the host, and assume positions of authority. Whenever he was host, he was appropriately one up; whenever he was a stranger or guest, someone else was appropriately one up. Examples of role-switching abound in the Gospels, and a careful reexamination of these encounters of Jesus would show just how versatile and subtle his ministry was.

THE STRANGER ON THE ROAD

The two companions en route to Emmaus are portrayed as insiders: they appear to know where they are going and they are traveling as a pair, perhaps a couple: Cleopas and an unnamed (and thus, perhaps, a woman?) companion. Maybe their conversation was so intense that they actually slowed their pace: in any event, Jesus caught up with them and walked alongside them. He is the stranger, the outsider to the group, and he asks them a question, which is a typical gesture or gambit of the one down or the outsider.

The first response of Cleopas is actually to identify Jesus as an outsider as if to clarify their respective social positions: "Are you the only stranger [*paroikos*] in Jerusalem who does not know the things that have taken place in these days?" [brackets added] (Lk 24:18). The word *"paroikos"* is one of the words for *stranger*. Whereupon, with appropriate deference, Jesus asks another question, and his potential hosts grace him with information. So far, the encounter shows the classic signs of conventional behavior and role-playing.

As soon as the insiders have told their version of the story, however, Jesus shifts abruptly from the deferential to the didactic: he will reverse the roles (which after all are still more implicit than explicit), in order to teach the disciples. As such he now becomes one up (teacher), and they become one down (learners). But, surprisingly, Jesus sounds disrespectful and is certainly unconventional as he addressed them as "You foolish [ones]." This could, of course, be the evangelist's license. In any event, they do not take offense: when they reach their destination and Jesus again does not presume upon their hospitality ("he walked ahead as if he were going on"), "they urged him strongly, saying 'Stay with us'" (Lk 24:29). Not only does he accept their hospitality, but once again he reverses the roles. It is the two companions—the word literally means sharers of bread—who again become guests and receivers, and Jesus the stranger who becomes the host, for he it is who took the bread and said the blessing, then broke it, and handed it to them.

What has happened is profound and not only in the more obvious "eucharistic" sense. It now transpires that Jesus had carefully laid the ground for this reversal of roles: the two companions acknowledge that in the course of the seven-mile walk[82] he had been explaining the Scriptures to them so intensely that their hearts burned with emotion. In that encounter, once again, Jesus was the teacher and they were the learners. In that encounter, the roles that were adopted informally when Jesus joined the group were now being rearranged in such a way as to allow Jesus to become the host of the evening meal. But most significantly, it was as a stranger that Jesus made his initial impact and left the most lasting impression. It was as a stranger that he brought them enlightenment, causing their hearts to burn. It was as a stranger— and this is a quite remarkable fact—that Jesus reinterpreted the events in their recent lives and helped them to understand their own complex and confused stories. For by the time "their eyes were opened, and they recognized him" he had actually vanished (Lk 24:31). They never explicitly knew him as Jesus, but only as the stranger.

Two dispirited disciples were utterly renewed by this encounter: they set out "immediately" and retraced the seven-mile journey. And they were not going to have the Eleven corroborate their story, but to proclaim to the Eleven what they knew to be true. Now they were on a mission, missionaries. Their near despair (they said "we *had* hoped") was replaced by real hope. As Dante reminds us, "without hope we live in desire," or in the words of Baruch Spinoza which might apply particularly to ourselves, "Faith cannot be without hope, nor hope without faith."

THE SON OF MAN IN GLORY

The second instance of Jesus as stranger is not only more familiar to many but has been badly misapplied by generations of Christians. The reasons are understandable: the more common application is actually easier and more congenial than the more appropriate one would be.

In the very final discourse before his passion and death, as recorded in the Gospel of Matthew, Jesus identifies himself as the Son of Man coming in glory and separating the sheep from the goats. This regal figure will allot rewards and punishment according to people's behavior. The critical phrase for us is "I was a stranger and you welcomed me" (Mt 25:35). On the strength of this, generations of Christians have taken it upon themselves to extend hospitality to strangers as a sign of Gospel hospitality in the modest hope of being counted among the blessed.

It is, of course, entirely consistent with the ministry of Jesus to show hospitality and kindness to strangers, and it is highly appropriate for disciples of Jesus to do the same. Keep in mind, however, that the one who makes the stranger welcome is also superordinate, while the recipient of hospitality (the stranger) is one down. The one who offers kindness also holds power and initiative, and the subordinate who receives may also become highly resentful of the one who gives.

In casting themselves as donors or almsgivers, some Christians have created and maintained asymmetrical relationships that have demeaned the people they serve and elevated their own status or self-importance. Saint Vincent de Paul said that we should pray that the poor will forgive us for the bread we break for them: in other words, our acts of kindness can sometimes be immoral. Marcel Mauss said something similar: "Charity wounds the one who receives; and our whole moral effort is directed toward suppressing the unconscious harmful patronage of a rich donor."[83]

What is useful to remember about the dynamics of giving and showing kindness to strangers is this: what can be highly necessary can also become highly patronizing; what is often given freely is sometimes received unfreely (since some recipients are not free to refuse); what is an expression of genuine hospitality is also an expression of superiority and control. What can we do about these circumstances?

The obvious answer is that we should examine how Jesus himself does it: he alternates between being the giver and the receiver, the host and the guest, the insider and the outsider, the one up and the one down, the master and the servant. The less obvious answer is to look again more carefully at the verse from Matthew's Gospel: "I was a stranger and you welcomed me." Jesus is saying that he himself took on the one-down, subordinate, outsider, needy-person, role. Therefore if *we ourselves* are to do what he did, then it is simply insufficient for us to take on the one-up, superordinate, insider, benefactor role. If Jesus identifies himself as the stranger then so must we.

We cannot do that unless we step across the boundaries and borders that insulate our lives and help us remain as insiders and in control. This imperative, therefore, requires us to go from where we are to where we are not, from the center to the edge. The mark of a Christian is to be engaged in a centrifugal outreach. We are called to turn our lives "inside out" (for others and from a sense of social duty), not "outside in" (for ourselves and in defense of personal rights). Today's vital and growing Christian parishes and communities are those that are turned out to face and embrace the world: this is mission. Today's moribund and shrinking parishes and communities are those that are turned in upon themselves and concerned about their own personal and fiscal survival: this is maintenance. A preoccupation with maintenance is killing our communities, imperiling mission, and stifling the Spirit.

Not only did Jesus identify himself as a stranger, but he gave instructions that his followers do three very significant things that might help them to act in a similar way. Sadly, it seems, we have overlooked these instructions, much as we have overlooked the implications of Jesus as stranger. In Matthew's Gospel, Jesus instructs his disciples to be both giver and receiver, both one up and one down. First he says, "Give to everyone who begs from you, and do not refuse anyone who wants to borrow from you" (Mt 5:42). Here the disciple is the donor who is one up. Then Jesus says, "Ask, and it will be given you" (Mt 7:7), and now the disciple becomes the recipient who is one down. The passage continues: "Search, and you will find; knock, and the door will be opened for you. For everyone who asks receives, and everyone who searches finds, and for everyone who knocks the door will be opened" (Mt 7:7–8). How many of us, however, affect the kind of self-sufficiency that precludes us from asking, seeking, or knocking—perhaps from an instinctive avoidance of being in the one-down position and of assuming the recipient status that such a position would imply. After all, those who ask are admitting their ignorance, those who seek acknowledge that they are lost, and those who knock are outsiders: no one knocks when they are inside their own domain.

So perhaps in this passage Jesus is instructing us, again, on the attitude required of us who are ignorant, lost, and outsiders. No wonder some of us resist.

Let us turn back to the specific issue of our willingness to be strangers. Here again, there are probably at least three plausible reasons for our hesitation. First, we would not, except by accident, want to find ourselves in the "stranger" role. Second, our culture and socialization processes form us to be self-reliant and responsible. Third, and perhaps the most important of all, we can see no redeeming features in being in the role of stranger; we only see strangers as *lacking* something, as deficient, or in a negative light. If that is the case, we will not be able to understand the significance of the Emmaus story, and certainly we will overlook the significance of Jesus saying "I was a stranger."

In our zeal to respond to Jesus the stranger by casting ourselves in the role of savior, we may have missed the implications: that we are called to be *as he was*, and that being a stranger was an intentional part of who he was. He did not cling to his equality with God but emptied himself. He was born as an outsider, chose to live as one, and accepted the ultimate humiliation of crucifixion outside the gate or city wall: the quintessential mark of the outsider. Even at a rather simplistic level, we can acknowledge that stranger is indeed one of a pair, stranger/host: strangers need hosts or donors, but donors and hosts also need strangers. This pairing which is important not only at the self-evident level but at the broadest cultural level, merits serious consideration.

THE POSSIBILITIES OF STRANGERS

The Letter to the Hebrews is quite clear: those who follow Jesus have here no abiding city. His crucifixion outside the gate stands as a challenge and reminder to us. Here is the relevant passage:

> Jesus also suffered outside the city gate in order to sanctify the people by his own blood. Let us then go to him outside the camp and bear the abuse he endured. For here we have no lasting city, but we are looking for the city that is to come....Do not neglect to do good and to share what you have, for such sacrifices are pleasing to God (Heb 13:12–14, 16).

To embrace the status and role of the stranger is to embrace ambiguity, uncertainty, surrender, and vulnerability. Jesus did it, and so must we. Yet in this very *kenosis* (self-emptying, one-down, subordinate status), mission itself becomes possible, God becomes all in all, the empty vessel becomes filled, the receiver becomes a giver, and the outsider is encountered and embraced. Jesus did it, and so must we.

Here are eight possibilities for whoever is willing to learn to be a stranger. They identify eight values the stranger can embody, eight gifts the stranger—and only the stranger—can contribute. As we consider them, not only might we see that strangers are not lacking in virtue or unable to contribute to communities, but that strangers can be critically important to the welfare of communities.

First, the stranger or outsider has a different history and life experience from the host or insiders. This difference is not claimed as superiority but is simply acknowledged. But since outsider and insider have, in the course of their different lives, been struggling with at least some common issues, the stranger may be able to share particular experiences with the insiders, and to the benefit of both.

Again, the stranger has different, though not necessarily superior, resources and even may possess actual solutions to some common problems. If the stranger is gracious and patient, it may be possible to share such resources and solutions, to the parties' mutual benefit.

Third, as the stranger crosses the threshold, entering a previously existing and relatively closed and compact world, so the stranger actually expands that world simply by virtue of being there. More technically, the stranger serves to open up the local microcosm; the stranger is the catalyst for change to the status quo. Most of us have certain set ways of doing things, especially if they seem to work efficiently. The stranger brings the possibility of alternatives: something not to be underestimated. People may always have interpreted certain ills as due to witchcraft or understood certain of their number to be possessed by demons. The stranger may gently offer other possibilities that would account for these ills but in ways not identified by the insiders. The alternatives that the stranger suggests can also help local worlds to move gradually onto a more global stage.

Another advantage a stranger may bring is perhaps less dramatic but surely no less important. Some communities find themselves demoralized, cut off, or in some kind of crisis. Their morale is low, and they find it difficult to become motivated the way they once were. In such circumstances, the presence of a stranger may act as a fillip, a boost to their confidence, and a strong injection of moral support. This source of renewed energy then gives the local community some of the motivation and courage it needs to continue. A stranger, in the right place at the right time, has the ability to convince local people that he or she would truly not want to be anywhere else in the world, nor with anyone else in the world at this time. This assertion can be more than flattering: it can be life-giving. It seems very close to what Jesus was alluding to when he said, "No one has greater love than this, to lay down one's life for one's friends" (Jn 15:13). Laying down one's life in this sense is not dying for others but living for others. It is something a stranger has a unique capacity to accomplish.

Fifth, every culture needs appropriate strangers. Every culture needs appropriate strangers. Those who imagine they are self-sufficient and that they can close their borders and exclude all outsiders have already signed their death warrant. Hubris, or overweening pride, comes before a fall. There will always be some tension between the one-up status of the insider and the one-down status of the stranger. But with careful handling, and appropriate deference and dialogue on the part of the host, the inequalities can be addressed and a relationship of greater equality and mutuality can be established. Strangers can be assimilated, at least to a degree. But though both parties may benefit from that assimilation, they also lose something as well: mutuality is, after all, give and take.

Following closely from the previous discussion is this point: a stranger is to a community as a blood transfusion is to an individual. The stranger can be potentially life-giving; yet blood is sometimes contaminated and transfusions have been known to kill people. This analogy illustrates the essential ambiguity of strangers and helps us understand why the host may need to establish some distance and why mutual relations are best developed rather slowly.

Seventh, sometimes communities are riven by internal dispute or factionalism. The stranger who has been part of a community for a while may become well-enough known by all members yet in the pocket of none. In such cases, and assuming he or she is modest, supportive, and appropriately nonjudgmental, the stranger may be the ideal person to act as mediator or bridge builder between groups whose pride otherwise prevents reconciliation between them.

Finally, it is important, having identified the sometimes overlapping gifts and opportunities a stranger brings, to reiterate the importance of a stranger being just that: an outsider, strange, not fully assimilated. Some people appear to think that they must at all costs shed their status of stranger and become one of the group as soon as possible. This is naive, or arrogant, and certainly implies the use of undue pressure. Important virtues of every appropriate stranger include readiness to surrender the initiative, willingness to allow someone else to have control, and trust that the relationship will develop reciprocally and with mutual satisfaction. This is evidently a tall order and perhaps a major reason why relatively few people succeed in becoming appropriate strangers. Those who must be in control, who cannot ask, seek and knock, will never be capable of *kenotic* ministry. It is ironic, perhaps, that a fully assimilated stranger (actually a contradiction in terms) would lack the prophetic potential of the more marginal, ambiguous, challenging, personally disinterested stranger, who is nevertheless relevant, life-giving, and committed to the community.

Can we, Christians in a post-Christian world—many of whose people are exploited, forcibly marginalized, victimized casualties of unjust systems—attempt the kind of self-emptying ministry that Jesus exemplifies? Can we attempt to live a preferential option for the poor and needy, the nobodies and the forgotten, not forgetting the privileged "number ones"? And can we do all this with generous hearts and a boundary-breaking commitment? Can we move to the edge of our comfort zones and communities and continue to do so until we die, always encountering people with the vulnerability of a stranger and the life-giving promise of Jesus? If so, we will be bearers of good news indeed, and Christianity will continue for another millennium after Christendom, or until the Son of Man returns.

SUMMARY

Perhaps most of those who read this book probably come from the so-called First World. Such a social location may serve to prick the conscience of the introspective and call us to greater responsibility for those whose circumstances are perhaps more precarious than our own. That is undoubtedly a good thing. However, many First World people remain either relatively unaware of the rights and needs of millions of their less privileged brothers and sisters, or satisfied that they "give to charity" or otherwise redistribute some of their own substance. Some of us may be among their number. This chapter has been an invitation to a much more radical living out of our Christian vocation. It argues that we must model ourselves on Jesus. Jesus deliberately "emptied himself" on behalf of others, and sought out the lowliest people and places. He located himself away from the comfortable center because that is where the marginalized and dispossessed were to be found. Having encountered them, he put himself at their service and did not simply bestow things on them in the manner of a patron or benefactor.

To move from the center to the edge, to exchange a position of authority and control for one of low-status and service, is to contribute to a rearranging of the world and a restructuring of relationships. In this world the first becomes the last, the master becomes the servant, and the teacher becomes the learner. And in that moment, that movement, the person who was overlooked and disenfranchised is raised up and dignified and the realm of God breaks through.

By intentionally moving between different perspectives (insider and outsider, host and stranger), we become more aware of the ambiguity, the challenge, and the potential of radical discipleship. Then perhaps, we can revisit the Emmaus story (and indeed all the post-Resurrection stories, which depict Jesus as stranger), as well as the climactic account of the Last Judgment and the end of Matthew's Gospel. Having pondered more deeply the example and invitation of Jesus, perhaps we ourselves are better placed to understand and follow.

Afterword

I f we think of the body of Christ as composed of each separate individual baptized Christian, then that body has an uncountable number of members. If we think of the historic fragmentation of Christianity, we will have to visualize a body that has been battered, scarred, and wounded. We may even see it as a body at war with itself.

Christians united by the same Creeds and believing in the same Jesus Christ are actually more similar than different, and more like siblings than neighbors. It is important, both for Christians and for the rest of the world, that we support one another in a common faith, even as we continue to address what separates, scandalizes, and divides us. It may not be helpful to minimize some of the very real differences between Christians, but we should surely maximize some of the similarities. Nor should we be unaware that there are sometimes more differences of opinion, understanding and practice, *within* a single Christian denomination, than there sometimes are *between* denominations. The ultimate criterion of authentic Christianity is not universal agreement on propositions, but outreach, reconciliation, and love. In short, it is time for Christians of good will to stand up and be counted, to galvanize themselves, to take the missionary dimension of their lives seriously, and to live up to their common baptism.

These pages are simply an invitation to a renewal of discipleship, and an appeal to radical Christianity in the footsteps and in the Spirit of Jesus, who prayed that his followers be one *in Him*. We may not be one in visible, institutional unity for some time, though there are encouraging signs in many of the churches and impressive agreements on matters of faith and practice. The Roman Catholic church may be among the very last to endorse in practice what it espouses in principle. We do not need to wait for formal agreements, but we do need to choose, to encounter, and probably to suffer. We need to do it together, and we need to do it now. Our salvation depends on it, the credibility of the Church stands or falls by it, and a world in need of Good News and nurture cannot be deprived of it any longer. God is gently and persistently disturbing us every day. It is time for us to go and do likewise.

Notes

Foreword

1. David B. Barrett, (ed.), *World Christian Encyclopedia: A Comparative Survey of Churches and Religions in the Modern World, AD 1900–2000*. New York: Oxford University Press, 1982: 820.
2. Christopher Dawson, *Medieval Essays*. Doubleday: N.Y., 1959. "Those [first] thousand years saw the making of Europe and the birth and re-birth of Western culture; they also witnessed the creation of that socioreligious unity that we call Christendom" ("The Sociological Foundations of Medieval Christendom," *op. cit.* 52–69). This quotation, p. 52.

Introduction

3. From a talk on the Holocaust by Michael Berenbaum, at Catholic Theological Union, Chicago, April 1998.
4. William Wordsworth (1770–1850), "Lines Composed a Few Miles Above Tintern Abbey" (line 88ff).
5. Viktor Frankl, *Man's Search for Meaning*. New York: Pocket Books, (1959) 1973.

Chapter One

6. Peter Millar, "Visions of Integrity and Transformation: Contemporary Challenges to the British Churches." D. Min. Thesis. Catholic Theological Union, Chicago, Ill., 1999.
7. We will consider this in greater detail in Chapter Four.
8. Thompson's image is particularly striking when one recalls his own struggle with drug smoking, and the fact that charcoal can only be made when the wood is prepared both by extreme heat and a complete lack of air. Thompson's own near-asphyxiation—both poetic and physical—is painfully evoked in these lines.
9. Genesis House, founded in 1984 by Edwina Gateley, continues to support women trying to escape from various addictions, and to treat them both professionally and with great love.

10. Thompson was famous, or notorious, for coining and adapting words. Here, the word "dravest" is a strong past tense of the verb *drive*. In earlier lines he uses the archaic word "limn," for *draw*.

11. We will consider this in more detail in Chapter Five. We note that the author of Matthew's Gospel, addressing a particular first-century community, and having a particular message to communicate, asserts that Jesus restricts the ministry of the Twelve to "the lost sheep of the house of Israel," and orders them not to turn your steps to pagan territory (Mt 10:5). Furthermore, Jesus is quoted as saying to the Caananite woman, "I was sent only to the lost sheep of the house of Israel" (Mt 15:25).

12. See the SEDOS Seminar, Final Report. In Jenkinson, W. and H. O'Sullivan (eds.), *Trends in Mission*. Maryknoll, N.Y.: Orbis, 1991: 399–414.

13. Rodney Stark, *The Rise of Christianity*. Princeton, N. J.: Princeton University Press, 1996.

14. Alan Kreider, *The Change of Conversion and the Origin of Christendom*. Philadelphia, Penn.: Trinity Press International, 1999.

15. This theme is developed in my essay "Belief and Faith, Assent and Dissent," *New Theology Review*, 1989: 65-85.

16. Paul III (Alessandro Farnese), pope from 1534 to 1549, lived through one of the most tumultuous periods of church history and distinguished himself in a number of ways. Not only did he declare the inhabitants of the New World to be human (1537), but he excommunicated King Henry VIII (1538), inaugurated the Counter-Reformation (1540), confirmed the Foundation of the Jesuits (1540), instituted the Inquisition in Italy (1542), and convened the Council of Trent (1545–1563).

17. James Scherer, "Bartholomäus Ziegenbalg." *Missiology*, 4, 1999: 487–94.

Chapter Two

18. Abortions total 40 percent of live births recorded in the U.S. (1997).

19. José Comblin, speaking at the Mission Institute, Lutheran School of Theology, Chicago, April 2000.

20. We will examine this more systematically in Chapter Five.

21. Gary Macy, "The Eucharist and Popular Religiosity," *Treasures From the Storeroom: Medieval Religion and the Eucharist*. Collegeville, Minn.: Liturgical Press, 1999: 172–195. The author carefully explores "the possibility that no absolute distinction between laity and ritually ordained existed before the late twelfth and early thirteenth centuries" (p. 173), and notes that the earliest argument against women's ordination is around 1240 (p. 175). "Historians and theologians should not assume that references to the "ordained" or even to priests earlier than the late twelfth century always refer to a permanently and ritually ordained group of males" (p. 175).

22. See John Wijngaards' Web site: www.iol.ie/~duacon/wompr.htm.

23. Apostolic Letter on Ordination and Women, *Ordinationis Sacerdotalis.* Dated May 22, 1994. *Origins,* June 9, 1994: 49, 51–2.

24. In Mary Ann Fatula, *The Holy Spirit, Unbounded Gift of Joy.* Collegeville, Minn.: Michael Glazier Books/Liturgical Press, 1998: 102.

25. "2001 and Beyond: Preparing the Church for the Next Millennium." Thomas J. Reese, S. J., *America,* June 21, 1997 10–18. This quotation, p. 13.

26. My *Random House* dictionary describes magisterial with the following adjectives: commanding; authoritative; domineering; dictatorial.

27. We only have to talk with younger Boomers or Generation Xers to realize how archaic and self-serving these titles sound today. Not that post-Boomers are totally wise, but they are certainly not naive; and clerical posturings have little or no effect on them.

28. *The Tablet,* May 2, 1998: 565.

29. The *World Christian Encyclopedia* (D. Barrett, ed.) for 2000 gives the figure as 33,820. See vol. I, 10.

30. A favorite quotation from Cameroonian theologian Eboussi Boulaga.

31. A fine book on the subject is by John Boswell is *The Kindness of Strangers: The Abandonment of Children in Western Europe From Late Antiquity to the Renaissance.* New York: Pantheon, 1988.

32. Roman citizens who were male heads of households *(paterfamilias)* had the right to decide whether a newborn child would be accepted into the family or rejected and abandoned.

Chapter Three

33. In languages beyond the Romance family (those derived from Latin), and beyond the Indo-European, there are other moods, tenses, and verb forms that would also offer possibilities for our thought experiment.

34. Jung Young Lee, *Marginality: The Key to Multicultural Theology.* Minneapolis, Minn.: Fortress Press, 1995.

35. Arthur D. Nock, *Conversion: The Old and the New in Religion From Alexander the Great to Augustine of Hippo.* London: Oxford University Press, 1933: 9–10.

36. The diagram here is adapted from the Bernardin Lecture given by sociologist Bryan Hehir, S. J., at Catholic Theological Union, Chicago, November 1988.

37. *Origins,* 1986: 477.

38. David Steindl-Rast, in *Fugitive Faith: Conversations on Spiritual, Environmental, and Community Renewal,* (ed.) Benjamin Webb. Maryknoll, N.Y.: Orbis, 1998.

39. I have taken the first eight of these, with some amendments, from Warren Bennis and B. Nanus, *Leaders: The Strategies of Taking Charge.*

New York: Harper & Row, 1986, in Charles Handy, *The Age of Unreason*, Boston: Harvard Business School, 1989: 134–5.

40. Joan Chittister, *The Fire in These Ashes*. Kansas City, Mo.: Sheed and Ward, 1995: passim, but especially 37–8, 67, 162.
41. David Nygren and Miriam Ukeritis, "Executive Summary of Study on the Future of Religious Orders in the United States." *Origins*, September 24, 1994: 258–272.
42. Hugh Mackay, *Turning Point: Australians Choosing Their Future*. Macmillan, 1999:137–138. Also, 103, 134.

Chapter Four

43. Gerd Theissen, *Social Reality and the Early Christians: Theology, Ethics, and the World of the New Testament*. Minneapolis: Fortress Press, 1992: 82, 91–2.
44. Nygren/Ukeritis, *op. cit.*
45. Nygren/Ukeritis, *op cit.* 270 (Conclusions).
46. These quotations are taken from Chapters 14, 15, and 16 of John's Gospel.
47. This is the title of Rodney Clapp's excellent book: *A Peculiar People*. Intervarsity Press, 1996.
48. One of Joan Chittister's finest books, for me, is *The Fire in These Ashes* (Kansas City, Mo.: Sheed and Ward, 1995). She develops the theme of overnight fires, though her point is not quite the same as my own here.
49. See Chapter Six for further development of this theme.
50. "People are marginalized when their membership in two groups poses a contradiction or cross-pressure such that their status in each group is lowered by their membership in the other." Rodney Stark, *The Rise of Christianity*, Princeton, N. J.: Princeton University Press, 1996: 52. This is what others have referred to as *active marginalization*, in distinction to *passive marginalization*, which can either be marginalization due to the fact that one simply has no freedom of initiative, or that one remains intransigent in the face of change. A vagrant may be passively marginalized; so also may a figure like Archbishop Lefebvre, who was unable to accede to the reforms of Vatican II. Active marginalization is exemplified in the choices Jesus made. We will consider it more directly in the next chapter.
51. This is the subject of Chapter Five.
52. Torpor is apathy, sluggishness, or lethargy. The second meaning in my dictionary is pertinent: "(of a hibernating animal) dormant; having greatly reduced metabolic activity."
53. There is some variation, with women's life expectancy as high as eighty-three years, and men's up to seventy-nine, in different countries.

Chapter Five

54. Such categorization, or distinguishing lines, can very easily come to be understood as marking real or actual distinctions ("Men *are* superior to women"; Muslims *cannot* be saved," and so on).

55. Even in a totalitarian system there is no such thing as a "one-man show." There is always need for a cadre of executives and implementers.

56. This will be pursued in Chapter Seven.

57. John Meier's multi-volume work is entitled *A Marginal Jew: Rethinking the Historical Jesus.* New York: Doubleday, 1994.

58. John Meier, *op. cit.* vol I: 303.

59. Matthew refers to *paidia, children,* while Luke, even more radically, speaks of *nêpioi, infants.* Strictly speaking, an infant is one without language: literally a voiceless one.

60. Kenan Osborne, *The Resurrection of Jesus: New Considerations for Its Theological Interpretation.* New York: Paulist, 1997: 152.

61. See Gerda Lerner, *The Creation of Patriarchy.* New York: Oxford University Press, 1986.

62. See *Societies at Peace: Anthropological Perspectives.* Signe Howell and Roy Willis (eds.). London, N.Y., Routledge, 1989.

63. It would be too easy to cite apparent counter-examples to this. But in virtually every instance of women's authority, it is either held by women acting as (social) men, or only by permission of men, or in situations that are considered insignificant.

64. General Colin Powell, Commander of the U. S. Forces in Iraq in 1990 said this "We bring young men and women into the armed forces to be warriors...in a warrior culture. They are not social workers. They are warriors. What is a warrior? Someone who can coldly intend to isolate the enemy and kill it." Notice how the General implicitly claims legitimation for the armed forces, and how he depersonalizes "the enemy" ("it"). The General is highly respected and presents himself as a Christian. Jesus, we recall, said something different: "You have heard that it was said. "An eye for an eye and a tooth for a tooth." But I say to you, Do not resist an evildoer. But if anyone strikes you on the right cheek, turn the other also"(Mt 5:38ff).

65. This, of course, depends on how or whether one differentiates among the nonparticipants. Women have indeed been treated as immature or deviant or both, whether or not they have been formally classified as such.

66. Technically, a role is an undertaking or activity consistent with one's status, while a status is an entitlement to play a particular role, or a social position associated with a role. Roles may be separated from status, as when someone pretends to be a police officer, and status may be separated from role, as when royalty waits on tables. The Roman

Catholic church maintains that women can never claim or enjoy the status of clergy. Jesus did not cling to his divine status but emptied himself and became as we are.

67. In 1682 Cardinal Laurent Bracanti at the College of *Propaganda Fide* in Rome, said this "The [missionary's] unique function is to preach the Word of God and his commandment, that is why they are sent, *missi....*Who, then, can be missionary?" The reply comes as an obvious axiom: none but men. All women are to be excluded from this function and will never be able to aspire to it. The work of the missionary is to preach. Preaching is a work of wisdom. Wisdom is not commonly found in women. According to Aristotle, *sapientia non viget communiter in muliereribus.* Cited in Pierre Charles, "Missiologie antiféministe," in "Le rôle de la femme dans les missions; rapports et compte rendu de la XXème semaine de Missiologie de Louvain, 1950." (Bruxelles: Ed. Universelle/Paris: Desclée de Brouwer, 1951): 20–21.

68. One thinks of various categories of people who, until very recently, have been excluded from access to the sacraments due to physical or theological barriers. But people who are physically incapacitated or mentally challenged are not thereby to be excluded from church or kingdom. Persons with Williams Syndrome are described as "instinctively caring and compassionate" but also "defective" and "handicapped." One physician spoke of them thus: "They cannot tell a lie. They are infectiously happy. They are concerned about others." Some set of handicaps! Of such is the realm of God.

69. The Vatican II document *Lumen Gentium* [Dogmatic Constitution on the Church] comes across as condescending as it includes "the laity" as recipients of the help of "the church." It effectively identifies pastors as the givers and laity as the receivers. The former "represent the person of Christ" and "promote the dignity and responsibility of the laity" (para. 37). There is more than a hint here of the laity as *insider nonpartici- pants,* and of course the horizontal line between the quadrants #1 and #2 (fig. 5, p. 106) continues to be strongly felt in the new millennium.

70. Gil Bailie, *Violence Unveiled: Humanity at the Crossroads.* New York: Crossroad, 1995: 274.

71. I was recently taken to task by a citizen of the United States who maintained that his country was an exception, having been deliberately founded on democratic principles enshrined in the Constitution. He did not remember the early history of slavery, the time before universal suffrage, or the contemporary face of race relations in his country, not to mention the way law itself is flouted.

Chapter Six

72. I have used a number of sources for this section. Particularly interesting and helpful is Andrew Strathern, *Body Thoughts*. Ann Arbor: University of Michigan Press, 1996.
73. See Londa Schiebinger, *The Mind Has No Sex: Women in the Origins of Modern Science*. Boston: Harvard University Press, 1989: 104–112.
74. In the U. S. in the first third of the twentieth century, midwifery as a mainstream occupation of women practitioners was largely eradicated. But the influx of foreign-born women, and the presence of African-American communities ensured that it did not completely die out. From the 1930s on there emerged a new kind of midwife: the nurse-midwife. She combined the professional expertise of nurse and the informal skills of the midwife.
75. See p. 139 of this text and note 77 below.
76. *Charisms* properly understood are gifts that exist to be given away. They are given by the Holy Spirit to individuals or organizations ("communities"), *for the building up of the wider community.*
77. See Robbie Davis-Floyd in *Many Mirrors: Body Image and Social Relations*. Nicole Sault (ed.). Rutgers University Press, 1994: 204–233. These quotations, pp. 227 and 228.
78. Plato, *The Collected Dialogues*, (eds) Edith Hamilton and Huntingdon Cairns. Princeton, N. J.: Princeton University Press, 1969. *"Theatatus,"* #149–150. This quotation, 855.
79. Plato (427–347 B.C.); Aristotle (384–322 B.C.); Kant (1724–1804).
80. Betty Friedan, *The Fountain of Age*. New York: Simon and Schuster, 1993; see my *Reading the Clouds: Mission Spirituality for New Times*. Liguori, Mo.: Liguori Publications, 1999: 155–58.

Chapter Seven

81. See Chapter Five.
82. If Jesus caught up with the pair a mile or two out of Jerusalem, they would probably have been walking together for at least two hours before arriving in Emmaus.
83. Marcel Mauss, *The Gift*. London: Cohen and West, 1970: 63.